BETWEEN THE LINES
and
INSIDE THE ROPES

BETWEEN THE LINES
and
INSIDE THE ROPES

Randy McWilliams

Copyright © 2022 by Randy McWilliams.

Library of Congress Control Number:		2022913593
ISBN:	Hardcover	978-1-6698-3614-8
	Softcover	978-1-6698-3613-1
	eBook	978-1-6698-3612-4

All rights reserved. No part of this book may be reproduced or transmitted in any form or by any means, electronic or mechanical, including photocopying, recording, or by any information storage and retrieval system, without permission in writing from the copyright owner.

Any people depicted in stock imagery provided by Getty Images are models, and such images are being used for illustrative purposes only.
Certain stock imagery © Getty Images.

Print information available on the last page.

Rev. date: 08/16/2022

To order additional copies of this book, contact:
Xlibris
844-714-8691
www.Xlibris.com
Orders@Xlibris.com
842768

INTRODUCING RANDY McWILLIAMS

A NOBODY WHO BECAME SOMEBODY

I had my doubters from the very beginning!

A person who didn't have the background, education, the know-how, and had a strong historical sense of failure to be successful. A "NOBODY" working with professional athletes, nationally ranked amateurs, and nationally ranked juniors, universities, and colleges.

These people have a personal vendetta to make sure that a NOBODY starts showing better results than what they have shown working with athletes.

"WHO IS THIS GUY?" "What do you mean he washes dishes, works, and owns a restaurant?" Agents of athletes saying, "We are going to trust your potential future career with this guy?" Some of the athletes I worked with even had their families, agents, teams, or someone to observe what I was doing.

What I had that most people didn't have was the lifelong exposure of being surrounded by successful athletes and most importantly, my parents!

The three characteristics of an athlete are the physical/mental/emotional, and you cannot compete if you don't have the three! You identify what area needs to be addressed to get the results, and your career is measured as success or failure.

At the time it was unheard of to have someone who would travel the world and do so much.

When I shared with my parents that I was going to work a second job, they thought it was an evening restaurant or something in the service industry!

An embracing saying to apply with life, "You're only given moments of madness, and if you lose that, you're missing a lot"

In my approach, you need that to compete.

You in the service industry or with anything in life. "HAVING AN IMPACT ON SOMEONE'S LIFE!"

"CHALLENGES TO LIFE! RISK and REWARD!"

"YOU HAVEN'T FAILED BECAUSE YOU HAVEN'T REALLY TRIED TO SUCCEED!"

I was healthy, outgoing, and loved challenges! My biggest success is recognizing I needed to change my social habits. I eliminated my alcohol and drug use! The awakening call was when I made an appearance to "SAY NO TO DRUGS" for former first lady Nancy Reagan, and I had to "PRACTICE WHAT I PREACH." Thirty years of sobriety!

My parents were the ones that were the happiest because they saw the "SPARKLE WITHIN" me again! What was really sobering is that "I WAS MISSING MY LIFE" and decided to change in a positive way!

I would compete in a new sport called triathlons in the infancy stages against great athletes.

I would ride my bike tirelessly in the desert where I had just recently resettled. I just stayed busy, and started riding a bike distance daily.

I started out working with professional cyclists. I had two professional bicyclists from Boulder, Colorado. They stayed at my house for two weeks. We rode fifty to seventy-five miles a day when my schedule permitted.

They had just finished the Colorado professional championships. From Vail, Boulder, Estes Park, etc., I got so hooked that I flew to Colorado to specifically buy a professional bike from them.

I WAS DIFFERENT, and not afraid to try!

"WHAT DO YOU WANT?" I kept asking myself.

"TAKE THE SHOT, AT LEAST TRY SOMETHING?"

From Shakespeare's King Lear Act 5, it writes:

"HE DIES."

The GREATEST writer of literature writes:
"HE DIES."
So simple, but let's become alive.

Most people would not continue after coming to this dramatic conclusion and ending. Like winning and losing! This is where it all begins!

You have to rise to the challenges you face in a competition! That is why the players I work with are prepared to rise to the challenges. I evaluate their preparedness and foundation of their athletic ability, what the history and past records show against their competition, and build on their competitive foundation and base. Where we want to go, they put in the work, and I just assist!

"LIMITATIONS ARE SELF-IMPOSED."
"Hard work pays off!"
"Rise to the challenges!"

So let's turn the page and see what comes next! Let the next story begin! I hope you enjoy the insight.

*NOTE: Originally *Between the Lines, and Inside the Ropes* was 8 1/2 x 11, 500+ pages, with over 400 images, pictures, documents, testimonials, letters, recommendations, newspaper articles, magazine articles, tributes, tournament resorts, organizations, brochures, television, radio, with the greatest athletes, celebrities, politicians, musicians that support the numerous stories. All pictures are the property of Randy McWilliams.

Parents on tennis court/with CA entry fees

Photo of Mom and Dad/Mom resting head on Dad's shoulder

The motivation and purpose of this book are dedicated to two remarkable people: my parents. Yes, that is a common cliché people use to find their inspiration, and I am like everyone else, I guess.

My father played for legendary coach Amos Alonzo Stagg. Knute Rockne was quoted "All football goes through STAGG." My father was captain of Stagg's fiftieth-anniversary team. Stagg, "The Grand-old Man" of football said, "McWilliams is the greatest student/athlete I have ever coached." Pops was a three-sport athlete: football, basketball, and baseball. He was offered an NFL contract with Chicago Bears that paid $25 a week, and turned it down. He was a pitcher and played professional baseball with the great Joe Dimaggio. In basketball, he was an all-conference center.

"Jo-Babe," his nickname, went onto graduate school at COP, now the University of Pacific, and coached football and baseball. At the Pacific, he led the "Tigers" to their only league championship in baseball. Pacific named their "Tigers'" new stadium with a plaque in the home dugout after my father.

"Jo-Babe" is considered by the Pacific the greatest student to grace their halls. He is a hall of fame Pacific member in basketball, football, baseball, and academics.

DAD, HUGH, "JO-BABE" (COLLEGE NICKNAME), McWILLIAMS

Father sitting at the desk

He continued coaching at the collegiate levels at the United States Naval Academy, Annapolis, Maryland. He was an offensive coordinator and assistant head coach under Wayne Hardin, who he coached at the Pacific. My father coached two Heisman trophy winners: Joe Bellino and Roger "the Dodger" Staubach. Pops was an innovator and an offensive genius. "No Huddle Offense" and "Unbalanced Line." Unfortunately, other coaches who consulted with my father took credit for his ideas.

He met his better half as a graduate student teacher subbing for the tennis coach. Unknown to my father, a hot new female freshman student was nationally ranked in tennis who just lost in the California tennis championships. My mother had heard he was the man in the campus with women lining up to date him. Remember this is the late '30s. My mother decided to play "right-handed," she was a lefty, and challenged Pops to a match the following day with a wager, "If I win, you have to go to my sorority dance the next weekend." As the story goes to witnesses (all have passed away), she drilled him; 6–1; 6–2 as she played her game.

The two of them went to the sorority dance, and my mother decided to take up smoking that evening to "Jo-babe's" chagrin. The rest of the story is history.

My mother coached tennis at private schools in Palo Alto, and Atherton, California. Her most famous student was Shirley Temple.

In Palo Alto, she took up golf and became an outstanding amateur golfer. She played numerous tournaments in the infancy stages of the LPGA Tour as an amateur.

Both of my parents played every golf tournament available, public, clubs, etc. At one time, they held five husband and wife championships. My dad was a scratch, and Mom was a two-handicapper.

My father became so obsessed with his golf, he turned down a coaching offer from "Oakland Raiders" Al Davis. My father's focus was all about golf.

They were married for sixty-five years, and both died at eighty-seven years of youth. Words cannot describe my emotions for them. There is an old saying, "Words can describe the feelings from mind, but actions truly convey the feelings from the heart." They backed up everything they said!

A LITTLE HISTORY OF "RANDY'S CAFE" ALMOST THIRTY-FIVE YEARS

You got to be kidding?! Most have bet on me to fail in this business venture, opening a small cafe in eighty-six. The constant verbiage is due to my introverted type B personality, and the demands of being in a difficult business, I would fail!

The Harvard Business Review suggested this is NOT a business venture to enter in. Their statistics and research say 90% of all restaurants close within three years, and 80% close within five years.

This is a seasonal business, and I proved my doubters wrong!

I have spent almost half my life between these walls! Entertaining beyond your wildest imagination!

Our local newspaper, the *Desert Sun* has recognized Randy's Cafe as the breakfast/lunch business established and open longer with the original owner and original location. VOTE #1 in PALM DESERT for breakfast with a legitimate call-in write-in poll with the Desert Sun readers. (See poll enclosed at the back of the menu)

The youngest sibling of Irish/Italian/French parents, devout Roman and Irish Catholics, native Californians, Palo Alto/Stanford who discovered the Coachella Valley in the 1960s. From Palm Springs to PGA West, La Quinta.

Parents who were devoted to family, faith, business, and sports. Both hall of fame athletes.

Clint Eastwood once shared with me, "Life is timing, and experiences, take advantage of what life has to offer!"

People and clients always inquire about my background and how I became successful with athletes.

First, and most importantly, I inherited great DNA from my parents.

I have been blessed, fortunate, humbled, lucky, and honored to mentor, train, assist, and cross paths and given rare opportunities that are few and far between in life.

Being athletically competitive throughout, life allowed me to create innovative ideas and concepts, and introduce state-of-the-art athletic programs.

Remember, "Limitations are self-imposed!"

As a youngster, I grew up in a community where I would observe horses working in water, and I was a competitive swimmer. I then created additional ideas in track and field, beach volleyball, football, rugby, tennis, cycling, golf, skiing, boxing, karate, judo, lacrosse, baseball, and basketball to create the first cross-training specialist.

Then I brainstormed introducing elastic bands, resistance training devices, plyometrics, yoga, yoga breathing, pool aquatics, weight programs designed for fast/slow-twitch muscles, nutrition, footwork, sand footwork, cardiovascular, video, mental, emotional, physical, and spiritual programs.

Thomas Bonk, *Los Angeles Times's* sportswriter of the year wrote, "RANDY McWILLIAMS IS THE NEW TECHNIQUE GURU IN SPORTS."

The company who started to certify athletic/sports trainers were clients of mine as well as numerous others who took lots of my ideas for financial gain.

What was a common comment was that critics were revengeful. A *nobody* who became successful. Remember this is late '80s and '90s. The jealous haters, adversaries that resented me being successful. They were having nothing else to do! Still to this day, but I am a competitor, athletic with great athletic background *who rises to challenges*.

It all started with me very young. My parents were great athletes.

I rode a bike 20–30 miles every other day. I ran ten miles every other day. I swam as much as I could to ocean water, bays, pools, etc.

I was approached by a gal and asked if she could ride and work out with me? And I would get paid! She became the body double for Jacquelyn Bassett in the movie, *The Deep*. Robert Shaw, Nick Notle, and the opening wet T-shirt scene are her memorable moments. Then a tennis player named Big Serve Roscoe Tanner (153 Mph, Raul Ramirez, Pilot Pen) and I worked on his rehab with Dr. Frank Jobe, then a four-time NCAA champion golfer, Gary Hallberg (Wake Forest), and then hall of fame MVP major league baseball player George Breet, Kansas City Royals.

My Stanford connection goes way back. Pops with too many Stanford players. I played lacrosse for three years with the Stanford lacrosse team while in high school traveling the country to play. (Stanford finally recognized the team and started to award scholarships). I have worked and trained eight Stanford student/athletes who went into winning NCAA championships.

I played rugby as a walk-on at Hastings Law School.

I have had the opportunity and spent time with five U.S. presidents, numerous senators, governors, ambassadors, and various governmental leaders, charities, organizations, and groups.

In the entertainment field from Sinatra-Peck, Crosby-Hope, Eastwood-McQueen, and many more. Check out all the musician's pictures and comments throughout the cafe.

My greatest contribution has been working with student-athletes. I have worked as a coach, trainer, mentor, and friend in assisting over a hundred student/athletes in attaining college/university athletic/academic scholarships. I have accomplished more with student-athletes winning local DVL, CIF, NCAA, and professional than any other in the valley.

I am asked who I think are the greatest tennis players and golfers: Rod Laver (two calendar Grand Slams, a decade apart); Rafa, the greatest clay-court player; Fed, Sampras, Bjorg, the greatest grass-court players. Remember that Fed *never* beat Rafa at the French Open, Roland Garros. Novak will be the greatest of all time! Steffi Graf is the greatest of all time as she won a calendar slam and a gold medal in the Olympics. Serena is *not* even close!

Tiger has made lots of players and networks rich, but Jack Nicklaus is the GOAT!

I tried to play professional football as a wide receiver (team articles on the wall). Unfortunately, I could not maintain the weight that teams wanted me to report to camp. I was fast, had great hands, and in the best shape of my life!

Hollywood shot a motion picture in the cafe with big stars. They transformed the cafe into a French cafe. It never made it to the big screen and cannot figure this out. I was never paid for a location fee or for their thirty meals.

I became a national spokesperson for Go Green and Enerpath, a PSA announcement. Go to YouTube, type in "broadcast yourself," then type into the search engine "palmdesertenergy."

So a little nobody where people post fake news and crap with nothing close to the truth, where I have learned from my mistakes, and makes sure I teach what I have learned by reflecting on the past and with what not to do, and do positive affirmations, and having an impact on someone's life. As my late friend, Dan Fogelberg, sang, "Lessons Learned."

Life's great treasures await you. Don't be late. Seize the day and make your life extradentary. Have no fear and open up your heart to change. Being comfortable is not living. "MAKE the REST of YOUR life, the BEST of YOUR life." (JPS).

And the final thoughts come from the late Robin Williams, "You're only given a little spark of madness, and if you lose that, you're nothing."

From me to you, "Don't lose that, it keeps you alive."

Enjoy your visit, read the stories, check out one thousand pictures, make great choices, and take care of your health.

CELEBRITY DEFINED AND TIDBITS

People inquire with me to define what celebrity means:

Webster Dictionary: A celebrity is a condition of fame or broad public recognition and attention given to them by the mass media.

Urban Dictionary: A person who is full of themselves, and of self-delusion, hypocrisy, and attention-seeking. They have no idea what they are talking about and provide nothing practical to society. They think they are humanitarians because they give to charity.

Randy's Dictionary: We are all celebrities and defined by our actions in our own way. A saying applies, "Words can convey the thoughts from our mind, but actions truly convey the feelings from our hearts." Action speaks louder than words! Most celebrities are full of hot air, especially when they have to reach in their pockets deeply.

My parents were in social and sports circles that allowed for siblings to experience situations that were not available to other children.

My parents were a very "good-looking couple." Dad had some motion picture experience and was also used in many major print productions.

My first experiences with the media came at a very young age appearing with my parents in a newspaper print in the late 1950s. I also appeared on a rotating television show with other children on "Captain San Francisco" produced in San Francisco. Our cast was usually about twelve to fifteen children (including my sister) and normally, I wore Hawaiian shirts.

From a very early age, I had no comprehension of the significance of who these people were that my parents were friends with and associated with in a social setting.

I started being aware that these friends of my parents were special, from celebrities, sports athletes, and politicians.

My first memorable moment was meeting an actress at a Stanford University fundraiser. My knees buckled and my heart fluttered when I conversed with Barbara Hershey. She was only a few years older than me, but already had a career starting to blossom in Hollywood. I was a ragging hormonal high school student conversing with a gorgeous, sexy great body, who was flirtatious with me! She even introduced me to now hall of fame Louis "Satchmo" Armstrong. The iconic musician and I stumbled speaking because my attention was on this friendly gracious Barbara Hershey.

I played for the Stanford lacrosse club as a high school student. I was able to eventually play on the third attack line. We were comprised of lacrosse college and graduate students and "mois." It was different when approached by my friends about what my plans were for the weekend, and I would say, "I am traveling out-of-state to play a collegiate lacrosse game."

We had a fundraiser for the team on the Stanford campus auditorium featuring the world-famous Romeros, the royal family of guitars. Classical guitarists who performed on the Ed Sullivan Show and their unusual stance playing style; right leg extended at the same angle and the left foot jacked up on a stool and four guitarists playing in unison.

I worked the ticket booth to a sold-out performance. At the conclusion of their performance, I compared Pepe to be as masterful as the young Jimi Hendrix.

A few weeks later, I was able to present a Vietnam question and answer forum at my high school, Palo Alto High School. Both sides represented the pros and cons of the United States being involved in the height of the Vietnam war. The panel was evenly represented with military brass and activists opposing the war. The activists were headlined with David Harris and his wife Joan Baez, a Palo Alto High School graduate. Joan Baez had the most beautiful skin, and I told her that. Additional Palo Alto High School graduates include James Franco, Jim And John Harbaugh, "Pigpen" Grateful Dead, Lisa Jobs (Steve Jobs's daughter), Rik Babka, Davante Adams, Charles Brenner, Grace Slick, Randy Mcwilliams, and many more.

Then getting my feet wet in politics, I decided to help the 1968 campaign of Robert Kennedy. As a young twelve-year-old, I attended the Army - Navy rivalry football game in Philadelphia a few weeks after JFK was assassinated. Attorney general and brother to JFK, Robert Kennedy represented JFK and the Kennedy family at the game. My mother encouraged me to get up and introduce myself to Robert Kennedy, Caroline, and John Jr., which I did. Robert Kennedy was happy to know my father was the offensive coordinator and assistant coach of the Naval Academy. A time to remember the rest of my life.

Years later, I took the opportunity to be involved with "Young Democrats for KENNEDY." My brother woke me up to hear Robert Kennedy's victory speech at the Roosevelt Hotel, and Kennedy was shot and assassinated! I was stunned! My nickname for playing football in high school was "Rosie" after Roosevelt Greer who happened to subdue Sirhan Sirhan with Rafer Johnson. After Martin Luther King was being assassinated in 1968, it was a tumultuous year!

I use to attend the "BILL COSBY" celebrity tennis invitational at Pebble Beach. For one year, COSBY had to relieve himself while playing, and without a bathroom in the vicinity, he proceeded to grab a towel and an empty tennis ball can, he then wrapped the towel around his waist and did his thing. The crowd roared when he turned the ball can and emptied it. The players I worked and traveled with had just won Wimbledon and were #1 in the world in doubles. We were contacted about an exhibition at Riviera Country Club and we asked if we would like to participate in "SAY NO TO DRUGS" for NANCY REAGAN charity.

We happily accepted and attended with the former first lady, NANCY, and her husband RONALD REAGAN. I was all in when I heard JANE SEYMOUR, my favorite actress, and one of my all-time favorite movies that she starred in "SOMEWHERE IN TIME" with CHRISTOPHER REEVE. JANE SEYMOUR was stunning, social, and beautiful.

My guys played LA Open at UCLA, and I sat behind JOHNNY CARSON and his wife and friends at evening matches. An almost empty section is where we sat and was impressed with JOHNNY CARSON's knowledge of the game, and he was a good club player. KEVIN SPACEY came in with a woman friend, who was gracious and humble. We were packed, and he found the time to bring to my attention of a misprint of RONALD REAGAN'S name on the original program I had displayed from the movie *Knute Rockne, All American*. We had a good laugh. I felt that he was targeted to destroy his career; he was very, very nice to me. KRISTIN DAVIS, AARON "Breaking Bad" PAUL, and ALEXANDER "Tarzan" SKARSGARD were the group of actors. Nine in total. They laughed, joked, ribbed me, and told me I lived a sheltered life because I didn't recognize all of them; they knew most of the athletes I worked with displayed throughout my business, and they were all fabulous. It was the only time in thirty-plus years that I had armed security in my establishment. *One Flew Over the Cuckoo's Nest*, the movie starring JACK NICHOLSON and STEPHEN DORFF, who was a friend of a Palm Desert resident, was a down-to-earth guy, and his other close friend was WES HOLDEN, son of WILLIAM HOLDEN. These two guys were not pretentious and just low-key and very nice.

THE SINATRAS

A night to remember with the "Chairman of the Board," FRANK AND BARBARA SINATRA, BOB & DOLORES HOPE, GREGORY PECK, DINAH SHORE, AND 007 in Rancho Mirage.

One of the more memorable evenings I had was the night at the "SINATRAS'" compound in Rancho Mirage.

I was about to hit the sack after a busy day. I got a call from a women friend, Bonnie Haydon from New York, whose daughter Vanessa married DONALD TRUMP Jr., and they have five children, legally divorced in 2019, and was asked if I would like to have dinner and watch a movie at the "SINATRA" compound. I said, "Why not?"

We arrived through security, and BARBARA SINATRA was waiting at the door and greeted us radiantly.

We were escorted to the dining room table to join some of the guests. I happily joined Mr. & Mrs. BOB HOPE, Ms. DINAH SHORE, BOBBY MARX, son of Barbara's marriage to a MARX brother and a business partner of my women friend from New York and the SINATRAS.

Mr. SINATRA was curious who I was and inquired about my employment and background. I shared with him that I owned a small restaurant and worked with professional athletes. He lit up when I told him of my Sicilian Italian heritage from my mother's side (for the record I am Irish, Italian, and with French heritage) then all of a sudden, I became like an adopted son. He asked Mr. HOPE to exchange seats with me from the end of the table to sitting next to him.

After dinner, he wanted to give me a tour of his liquor room or cellar. Then we proceeded to venture into the home theater to watch a new release movie *True Believer*. The theater was unbelievable, with everyone having their own love seat sofas.

Throughout the movie, two gentlemen from behind me kept reaching over my shoulder from both sides helping themselves to my popcorn. I thought to myself, "Why don't they just ask for their own popcorn?" My other thought that it was way past my bedtime, midnight, and maybe they saw I was nodding off to sleep.

The movie concluded as the lights were slowly coming back on, then suddenly, as I was stretching my arms, a gentleman grabbed my shoulder abruptly from behind and said, "Thanks for sharing your popcorn, I'm 007." Then the other gentlemen pushed 007 aside and said, "Thanks for your popcorn I'm GREGORY PECK."

I was speechless as this surreal moment played out as my mind raced through the archives of all the movies these two have been in. They asked if I wanted to shoot the bull joining everyone else. So I had a wonderful night listening to stories, uncontrollable laughter, and emotions.

The SINATRAS' personnel assistant, Bobby, for over twenty years, was a former employee of mine. Mr. SINATRA told and directed Bobby to make sure I got to see his "Gold Record" collection before I left. As I was getting ready to leave at 3:00 a.m., Bobby said "Mr. SINATRA" wanted me to see his gold record collection. I said, "Where are you taking me?" Bobby said, "The collection is in the master's bedroom." I said, "No way!" Bobby insisted his job would be in jeopardy if Mr. SINATRA inquired if I saw his "Gold Record" collection. Bobby could not lie!

What a day and evening! On the tennis court with the great ROD LAVER—the "GOAT" of tennis in the morning, and a night to remember with SINATRAS, HOPES, DINAH SHORE, 007, and GREGORY PECK!

Our local newspaper *the Desert Sun* columnist wrote an article about my day and evening. The SINATRAS are very private people, and I will share future meetings with BARBARA SINATRAS. GREAT EVENING!

BARBARA SINATRA

Mrs. SINATRA has the "Barbara Sinatra Children's Center" at the Eisenhower Hospital campus in Rancho Mirage.

Every year, she has a fundraiser luncheon for her center.

I was a guest of the CEO founder of the BETTY FORD Center (I trained the CEO's son), and sat at his table.

The first luncheon was held at the Ritz Carlton in Rancho Mirage with the honored guest coach JOHN WOODEN and 700+ guests. Our table was located next to the honored guest's table, and Mrs. SINATRA.

When the opportunity allowed, I approached Mrs. SINATRA'S table and coach WOODEN. I refreshed Mrs. SINATRA'S memory about my visit in her home years earlier, and I was taken back by her remembering my name and asking me how my businesses were going? She also commented I looked happy!

Then she introduced me to Coach WOODEN. I told Coach WOODEN we had something in common. He looked curiously at me for a follow-up. I shared with him my father was a coach and captain of AMOS ALONZO STAGG'S fiftieth-anniversary team and considered

STAGG my father's mentor. AMOS ALONZO STAGG was basically a father figure to my dad.

Coach WOODEN had a sparkle in his eye and was moved by a reflective time gone by in his life. Coach WOODEN called STAGG his inspiration in his life. It brought back memories of a time gone by the parallels of these two men both lived to 100+, both lived by the teachings of the bible, never swore, and WOODEN credited some of his coaching lessons from STAGG.

Mrs. SINATRA and our paths crossed again at the next luncheon honoring JOE TORRE, New York Yankee and Atlanta Braves manager at Esmeralda in Indian Wells.

Once again, I approached Mrs. SINATRA and before I could say a word, she extended her hand and said, "Hi Randy, how is everything?" Then she turned to her friend, "I want to introduce you to YOGI BERRA/"

JAMES DEAN, STEVE MCQUEEN, BILL HICKMAN

Who is BILL HICKMAN? He was the first recognized superstar stuntman in Hollywood!

He and JAMES DEAN were best of friends. The two of them were driving up to Salinas with DEAN to participate in a race. DEAN was driving his Spider Porsche, and HICKMAN followed in his Ford. DEAN was driving his Spider Porsche and had a head-on collision with another vehicle. BILL HICKMAN was one of the first at the tragic accident scene and pulled Dean from the wreckage and sadly died in Bill's arms.

Bill Hickman was a close personal friend of my uncle, and he knew my father.

My father was asked by Bill Hickman if he would like to come up to the set of the movie *Bullitt* starring Steve McQueen. Bill was choreographing the action and driving the historic car-chase scenes.

After shooting the infamous car scenes in the street, Bill and my father returned home to Palo Alto to take my mother to dinner. My father drove his car while Bill waited to take my mother in his car.

My mother had no idea what a "stunt driver" was (unheard of at the time) and proceeded to meet my father for dinner. My mother asked about the day's movie sequences and he said, "Hold on, I show ya!" My mother was in almost a fatal accident in Palo Alto as Bill drove 60 mph, running stop signs and lights, and passing cars on the streets where her life almost ended. My father greeted them at the front of the restaurant, Mom was shaken and short of having a heart attack in her thrill ride! Bill's adrenalin was still trying to subside from *Bullitt's* earlier in the day car-chase scenes.

In the final days of shooting the movie, Mom got to meet McQueen, and she was proud to share her experiences with friends after the theatrical release of the movie.

Hickman went onto Oscar history over a three-year period with twelve Oscars. *Bullitt*, *Patton*, and the *French Connection*. His career ended in a stunt that went terribly wrong in the movie the *Seven-Ups* with an accident hitting a parked semi-truck going 60+ mph.

BEVERLY HILLIBILLIES, JETHRO AND JED CLAMPET

I lived in Lahaina, Hawaii, and worked in a restaurant where Buddy Ebson was frequent. I introduced myself and told him I was a big fan of the *Beverly Hillbillies*, and after my shift, we would chat. I started inquiring how he got started in the show business.

He shared that he danced with Shirley Temple in *Captain January* in the late '30s, and I told him that my mother had Shirley Temple as a tennis student in the bay area. He then told me he was originally given the roll of the "Tin Man" in the *Wizard of Oz*, but got deftly sick from the aluminum costume. Then I shared with him I had met Ray Bolger "Scarecrow" from the *Wizard of Oz* at the Bing Crosby Clambake golf tournament at Pebble Beach. He then opened up about his career and being a dancer.

Additionally, I also shared with him about meeting Max Baer, Jr. at the Bing Crosby Clambake. I was an ass though harassing "Jethro" with hillbilly slang and joking with him. I also tried to flirt and commented about Jethro's beautiful girlfriend. To say the least, he was not thrilled!

Buddy Ebson was a huge talent and a wonderful gentleman.

DUSTIN HOFFMAN

He also visited Lahaina, Maui, Hawaii, often.

I was never one to be shy when I would see someone who is a celebrity, or you would think unapproachable.

When I first noticed him, I thought he was bigger in life than his 5'7' height. *The Graduate* and *Marathon Man* are rated in my top twenty movies of all time.

So I approached him unexpectedly and surprised him by saying, "Look I invested in plastics, and looked what happened to me?" And I added, "And now I'm working in a restaurant." The first line was similar from *The Graduate* movie about what Benjamin Braddock might do in his future. He laughed out loud!

The following evening, I approached him again and whispered in his ear, "Is it safe? Is it safe?" from the thriller movie *Marathon Man*, where Dr. Szell played by Sir Lawrence Oliver.

He would come down to the beach from where he was staying and would watch us play beach volleyball—so down-to-earth!

"The Iconic" GINGER ROGERS

The "Golden Era" Oscar winner Ginger Rogers resided in Rancho Mirage. Ms. Rogers was a dancer, actress, and dance partner of Fred Astaire.

I approached Ms. Rogers and introduced myself while she was returning to her table at dinner. I asked her, "Could I have the next dance?" She said sure and placed her hand in my hand, and we slowly waltzed toward her table.

I kept the small talk at a minimum, and she commented she enjoyed meeting me and talking to me.

Someone approached me and said, "You should read her comments 'bout dancing with men."

"Part of the joy in dancing is a conversation, trouble is some men can't talk and dance at the same time."

Not with me.

CLINT "DIRTY HARRY" EASTWOOD

I lived in the Monterey area for a number of years and worked as a manager in the most popular bar/restaurant in Santa Cruz, California.

I was Christmas shopping and saw Clint Eastwood and his girlfriend at the time, Sandra Locke. Like always, I went up and introduced myself and he knew about the bar/restaurant I worked at and I knew about him owning the Hog's Breath in Carmel.

He was using filming at one of my friend's houses for sequences for his movie *Sudden Impact*.

Years later, I was invited to the opening of the "Carmel Ranch" where the new owners included Mr. Eastwood.

I approached Mr. Eastwood and shared with him that we met years earlier while we were shopping during Christmas in Santa Cruz. I then told him I had moved on and opened a small "Cafe" in the desert and worked with professional golfers and tennis players.

A few years later, I was caddying for a professional PGA Tour player at the AT&T tournament at Pebble Beach courses.

I was on the driving range getting my tour player ready for our tee time at Pebble. I saw Mr. Eastwood entering the range preparing for his tee time with his caddy.

I stopped briefly and said hi and wished him "Good luck and have fun today." He stopped looked at me curiously and he said, "How are you doing? How is the restaurant business treating you? Is this one of your pros?"

We exchanged wishes and I threw the bag over my shoulder and proceeded to the first tee and thinking how cool was that he acknowledged me!

CHARLES "PEANUTS" SCHULTZ AND HANK "DENNIS THE MENACE" KETCHUM

I was caddying in the AT&T Professional/Amateur golf tournament at Pebble Beach, California.

Each foursome has two professionals, and two amateurs playing three of Monterey's golf courses trying to qualify for Sunday's final round. The professional tries to qualify for the final round with his score on his ball, and a combined team score with his amateur to qualify. The amateur score is an adjusted handicap.

The rounds are long from five to six hours possibly. Sometimes, the amateur even though his score on the hole won't affect the team score, the amateur will play until he holes out, which is putting the ball in the hole. Amateurs pay up to $20K+ to have the privilege to play with marquee-named players.

So it is challenging to say the least. You are always backed up on the tee for the group in front of you even more so at "God's" golf course—Pebble Beach.

We had to wait for every hole at the tee box. When we finished our hole, the group ahead would be waiting to hit their tee shots. The amateurs in front of us were the two most famous comic strip writers on the planet. Charles "Peanuts" Schultz, and Hank "Dennis the Menace" Ketchum.

Normally, the professional partners would engage in conversation with playing partners. I noticed that neither one of their professionals was engaging in conversation with them. They were always sitting on the bench on the tee box conversing with each other.

So after seeing them as we waited, I finally broke the ice and said hi and introduced myself. Mr. Schultz overheard my player saying something about me being a trainer, which was unheard of at the time, and especially caddying. I was also a native Northern Californian like himself!

Mr. Schultz inquired with a curious exploring understanding of "What was meant as a trainer?" I shared with him that I work with athletes which have allowed me to travel the globe. From the courts of Wimbledon to the holes of Pebble Beach. We had animated conversations for a few days.

A couple of weeks later in Rancho Mirage, California, at the LPGA Dinah Shore Nabisco golf tournament, Mr. Schultz and I ran into each other again in the Nabisco Food Court Tent. Best tournament hospitality!

He greeted me with a radiant smile and asked me how I have been, and what was I doing here. I shared with him I was working with hall of fame tennis players and giving a clinic with Nabisco sponsors.

We shared laughs and great conversations. As I said goodbye, Mr. Schultz said, "Keep reading my strip." A few weeks later, the "Peanut's" Sunday strip had "Snoopy" as a trainer.

PAUL NEWMAN

PAUL NEWMAN and "FORSMMAN CO" had the "Huggy Bear," a unique format tennis tournament played in the backyards of his friends' houses in the Hamptons, New York. It originally started with friends playing doubles, the doubles became very competitive, and players started bringing in better players that eventually turned to bring in professionals, not club professionals but ATP touring professionals. The tournament was always played the bye week before the U.S. OPEN at Flushing Meadows. Newman and the tournament co-director would get all surfaces at backyard courts resurfaced at exactly the speed of U.S. Open tournament courts by the same open surfaces. The night before the tournament started, Newman hosted an extravaganza with the teams, schedules, and handicaps. What was unique is that you could buy your teams "bisques" or better known as points to use during your matches, then the gambling with odds on every team. My players were #1 in the world, and sometimes they made more money playing in NEWMAN'S tournament than winning a Grand Slam Doubles title. What was really fun was our accommodations were at various estates and mansions on the Hamptons! This tournament raised millions of dollars for NEWMAN'S "HOLE and the WALL GANG" charity and other NEWMAN charities. The tournament was marked given every year! PAUL NEWMAN'S brother ARTHUR NEWMAN, ninety-six, a philanthropist like his brother, lived in my hometown and passed away in December 2020.

TRIBUTE TO PARENTS
HUGH and Toni SOULMATES SIXTY-FOUR YEARS

WILLIE MAYS-BASEBALL

Growing up in the bay area, I was a big fan of the SAN FRANCISCO GIANTS baseball team, and WILLIE MAYS was a superstar of the talented roster team, the SAN FRANCISCO GIANTS.

One day at Aptos Seascape Country Club in the Monterey Bay area in California, WILLIE MAYS was playing golf with a few of his friends at the club. We were a twosome, my father and I, playing behind his group. We caught up with him on the fourth tee and WILLIE MAYS asked us if we would like to play with them because we were twosome and playing fast, and normal golf etiquette is to let the faster group play through. We decided to join their group for a few holes.

I still remember to this day, WILLIE MAYS hit a drive on a par 4, #6 where a large oak tree stood in the middle of the fairway. The tree split the fairways for your approach (second shot) to the green. WILLIE MAY's tee shot went over the highest part of the oak tree and landed just short of the green, 350+ yards. A towering shot. Today, that shot would challenge BRYSON DeCHAMBEAU length today off the tee box.

Our family condo was adjacent to the seventh green, par 3, where we ended our day playing with future hall of famer inductee WILLIE MAYS.

GEORGE BRETT-FRED LYNN-BASEBALL

FRED LYNN, who played baseball with the BOSTON RED SOX, BALTIMORE ORIOLES, SAN DIEGO PADRES, DETROIT TIGERS, and CALIFORNIA ANGELS in 1975 was an MVP and ROOKIE OF YEAR and a nine-time major league all-star. FRED LYNN had a home in Rancho Mirage, California, at Mission Hills Country Club, the host course of "DINAH SHORE and COLGATE, and ANA INSPIRATION" LPGA major, and he was a country club member. FRED LYNN was a fabulous athlete and very competitive. He watched my tennis training on the courts and throughout the facilities with some of the world's top tennis players. Our paths crossed on a regular basis at the club courts, gym, and the clubhouse dining area. He wanted to hit tennis balls with me, and we played tennis, and he smoked me easily. It wasn't fun. Over time, whenever I played tennis sets with someone, the opponent would always rise to the occasion because I trained, coached, and played with some of the best players in the world. My friendly social games were no longer fun, it was always like my friendly get-togethers would be like playing the finals of WIMBLEDON.

GEORGE BRETT, hall of fame baseball player for the KANSAS CITY ROYALS also resided at Mission Hills Country Club in Rancho Mirage. GEORGE BRETT was a terrific guy, very private and took his professional baseball off-season preparation seriously. Money future career implications were in place for his next two-year contract ($4–$8 million, what a deal to today's standards) we spent our days stretching, yoga, and he got into disciplined positions that he had no idea he could do. Yoga was relatively new to the professional athlete. We incorporated aqua/pool exercises to develop speed, flexibility, and strength for the upcoming season. GEORGE was in a new contract extension year for $4–$8 million with the KANSAS CITY ROYALS. Yes, $4–$8 million! A hall of fame baseball player making scratch compared to 2020+$$$!

I incorporated a program customized for him that would enhance his career. New ideas such as running, sprints, resistance, yoga, plyometrics, balance drills in the pool, and then incorporating GEORGE swinging a bat in the pool for a period of time. Starting working in the deep end and progressing to the shallow end with less water resistance which worked balance and speed through the strike zone, unheard of in the time, and worrisome to the KANSAS CITY ROYALS with their star and future hall of famer working with a local trainer. The results that season—he led the league in hitting his third batting title, but most importantly he tied for the league lead in doubles. He had forty-five doubles and tied JODY DAVIS of the BOSTON RED SOX. The pool work and cutting the angle approaching first base paid dividends. During the HOWARD COSSELL ALL-AMERICAN COLLEGE CELEBRITY GOLF TOURNAMENT at Morningside Country Club in Rancho Mirage, California, GEORGE seeks me out while playing. I was caddying for GARY HALLBERG, he enthusiastically approached me and shared with me how well he felt for the upcoming season. When GEORGE got engaged, he brought the future MRS. GEORGE BRETT by my business to meet me. GEORGE BRETT is a GOD-send to major league baseball.

HUGH AND STAN McWILLIAMS—BASEBALL

My father and his brother STAN McWILLIAMS who both played at COLLEGE of PACIFIC (UNIVERSITY of PACIFIC) as pitchers both signed contracts and were protected major league baseball players with the PHILADELPHIA ATHLETICS and BOSTON RED SOX during World War II. My uncle went on to play a few seasons with the BOSTON RED SOX, and my father decided to continue his education and pursue his master's degree and coach the COLLEGE of PACIFIC baseball team, and lead them to their only league baseball championship to this day. The new UNIVERSITY of PACIFIC baseball stadium dedicated and honored my father in naming the home team dugout to my father with a plaque in his honor located in the dugout.

STANFORD FOOTBALL

STANFORD UNIVERSITY football players JIM PLUNKET, DAVE TIPTON, and a few others of STANFORD UNIVERSITY varsity team football were noon-hour lunch supervisors at PALO ALTO HIGH SCHOOL directly located across the street from the university. The land where PALO ALTO HIGH SCHOOL (PALY), and its proximity location from the campus where MR. LELAND gave the land to build "PALY," is directly across from the football stadium and athletic fields, which made PALY felt a connection to the campus. On Saturdays at the old STANFORD UNIVERSITY gym in the early '70s there was pick-up 3–3 basketball games at the gym. JIM, DAVE, and ROD KEDZELL, and other STANFORD varsity football players played almost every Saturday. They dominated the court play. You had to sign up and wait your turn to play the "Winners" of the games. The late GEORGE BINGHAM, PAUL BURDICK (Superior Court Judge, Santa Cruz County), and myself were the only high school guys to defeat them a few times. We could flat out play ball. We were only a few years younger, and would we brag about Saturday exploits.

STANFORD TENNIS

DICK GOULD is the winningest NCAA coach, with seventeen titles, I can mention in the same class as JOHN WOODN, VINCE LOMBARDI, and my father. A class act who represents STANFORD UNIVERSITY well. I have been humbled and blessed to assist in contributing to STANFORD UNIVERSITY tennis by working with numerous players at the "Farm" (tennis chapter section).

OAKLAND RAIDERS

OAKLAND RAIDERS AL DAVIS offered my father a coaching position in 1969 with the AFL team which my father turned down so he could work on his golf game. The OAKLAND RAIDERS were an AFL team in the infancy stages of the league. AL DAVIS hired JOHN MADDEN who took the position offered to my father, then throughout the years, I had run-ins with OAKLAND RAIDERS football players and organization. OTIS SISTRUNK was a massive presence, his body looked like he had tree trunks for limbs. HOWIE LONG is another fabulous OAKLAND RAIDER, a father and a family man. I introduced myself to him at a restaurant in Ventura near Oxnard where OAKLAND RAIDERS had their preseason training camp. I remember extending my hand in a gesture of a handshake, and he extended his large hand. I noticed that his hand went limp and gentle into my hand like wet noodles. I inquired why that was different. He said everyone usually grips and squeezes my hand because of my size and being a professional football player, and he said, "This is now how I shake hands." JIM PLUNKETT was a gentleman, who was proactive and admired because he took care of his parents who were blind and they had a compassionate loving son who was there for them 24/7. JOHN MATUSZAK was scary especially when I met a flirtatious young woman who happened to be his girlfriend who was coming on to me at a bar. My new 2002 BMW allowed me to escape a pissed off MATUSZAK. JOHN ELWAY lived at the "FARM" (STANFORD UNIVERSITY) at the Angel Field House which is now a gift shop. He was on the list of QUARTERBACKS at STANFORD; JOHN BRODIE, STEVE DILS, the late DON BUNCE, GUY BENJAMIN, JIM PLUNKETT, and ANDREW LUCK, playing under various coaches who took each one of their games to a different level with great future success.

NFL

I had the opportunity to spend time with some NFL football players in Cancun, Mexico. I was invited to be an additional host at a real estate marketing investment seminar with about twenty-plus players and their agents. DENVER BRONCO'S players, STEVE ATWATER, big guy for a defensive back, recently enshrined at the NFL hall of fame in Canton, Ohio, and RAY CROCKET, both of these guys were great family men and class acts. It was funny to see these huge guys in bathing suits and speedos. I was body surfing at sunset when some players on the beach were motioning from the beach toward me. Little did I know that sharks cruise the brake at sunset and they saw a shark dorsal fin coming in my direction in the water. I thought they were motioning that a good set of waves were approaching. They were motioning to get out of the water, and come to shore. I thanked everyone profusely for motioning me to get out of the water before being eaten by a shark for the shark's early dinner. Our final night was eating at "Ruth Chris Steakhouse." Almost every player and agent personally thanked me for being myself and not a phony. Some of my all-time favorite NFL guys are EARL THOMAS, BEN DAVIS, AND PAUL WARFIELD, all three were regulars at my business, and I was introduced to all of them by WALT JENKINS of Houston, Texas, and Indian Wells, California. EARL THOMAS was one of three brothers who all played in the NFL at the same time. He was a motivating speaker, he loved his family, and was a terrific guy. He passed due to Covid-19. BEN DAVIS a quiet man. PAUL WARFIELD was a humble and reserved gentleman, surprisingly slight in size, but one of the greatest receivers in the history of the NFL.

HEISMAN TROPHY

My father was the offensive coordinator and assistant head coach at U.S. NAVAL ACADEMY. My father coached two HEISMAN TROPHY winners in a three-year period. JOE BELLINO and ROGER STAUBACH. STEVE BELICHICK, BILL BELICHICK'S father was my dad's offensive assistant at the NAVAL ACADEMY. The NAVAL ACADEMY football team between 1960 and 1963 had the HEISMAN TROPHY winner JOE BELLINO who played the MISSOURI TIGERS in the ORANGE BOWL and lost, and then the HEISMAN TROPHY winner ROGER STAUBACH and the number two college football team in the nation played DARRELL ROYAL and the number one team in the nation, UNIVERSITY of TEXAS and NAVAL ACADEMY lost. At the COTTON BOWL game was the first time the #1 and #2 teams played with a HEISMAN TROPHY winner. Back in the day, there were really only four bowl games: ORANGE, ROSE, COTTON, and GATOR bowls. And then today, "SPYGATE," with the NEW ENGLAND PATRIOTS wasn't new to BELICHICK with the team being fined and lost draft picks. Bill's father Steve and my dad would scout and secretly film upcoming opponents before they met back in the '60s. Bill learned to "SPYGATE" from our fathers.

BOXING

I have met a few world-class boxers. The late MARVIN "MARVELOUS" HAGLER while he trained in Palm Springs was a technician and very dedicated to his training and regimen. After his workout sessions, he would acknowledge the fans watching his workouts. OSCAR DE LA HOYA was shopping at a La Quinta grocery store early in the evening. I observed and watched numerous shoppers approaching him for autographs and pictures. I approached him and introduced myself, gave him a card, and spoke to him about everything except boxing. Golfing was a common subject since I lived at PGA West, and he played golf there earlier in the day. The following day, I read he was accused of sexual assault in Los Angeles that late night. I was shocked that he went back to Los Angeles that evening and got arrested. MUHAMMAD ALI, every athlete I worked with or didn't always said they were moved beyond description in meeting ALI. I followed ALI as a youngster fighting SONNY LISTON, listened on the radio during his first encounter with the feared heavyweight SONNY LISTON. ALI won! I could NEVER get enough of him, CASSIUS MARCELLUS CLAY, "FLOAT LIKE A BUTTERFLY, AND STING LIKE A BEE." His religious and personal beliefs that he had no qualms with the "Vietcong" and the UNITED STATES government took three years of his life during his peak boxing career taken from him and being able to return to the ring "THE GREATEST OF ALL TIME" with an unbelievable display of his talent. I went to a closed-circuit fight in Oakland for the "RUMBLE IN THE JUNGLE." The fight was in Oakland George Foreman's former home turf. I bet my friend that "ALI" would win against insurmountable odds. "THE ROPE A DOPE" was born, and the brilliant strategy fight with George Foreman was remarkable. I have continued to be an avid boxing fan. Boxing is similar to any competitive sports. In tennis you have a change over, similar to boxing, you adjust, adapt, evaluate strategies, change, and apply for a different or continued winning result.

SHAQ-WILT CHAMBERLIN–NBA

The summer of 1995, my ex-wife and I spent the summer traveling with a talented group of young tennis players. We spent a few weeks in Manhattan Beach, California, with the current number 1 doubles player in the world who I trained. We were honored to share the gym with NBA player KURT RAMBIS who lived at Manhattan Country Club. He was curious on the training programs that I was incorporating in our workouts: plyometric, explosive weight work for fast-twitch fibers, and slow-twitch fibers, yoga, aqua therapy, running in pool, and our running interval work. SHAQ O'NEIL lived in Manhattan Beach during the summer and daily rode a little motorized scooter to the courts in Manhattan Beach, and he was so massive you couldn't even see the bike. He played ball every day and had an acrobatic team where his sons would run up the back of his dad and leap toward the hoop receiving a pass from a teammate and then dunk the ball. It was a sight to be seen, a great father and an outstanding man.

WILT CHAMBERLIN-The GREATEST basketball center of all time!

Yes, BILL RUSSELL won more championships than any other center with the BOSTON CELTICS, but "WILT the STILT" with an average of over thirty points a game, and ten rebounds for his career. "WILT" even scored a hundred points in a game in Hershey, Pennsylvania. When you take the HERSHEY tour train, one of the stops is at the sporting venue where he accomplished the feat.

WILT wrote a book where he was quoted that he slept with over twenty thousand women, even shared with the public, "60 MINUTES," his bachelor pad in the hills of Los Angeles.

In the summer of mid-seventies, I lived in Santa Cruz and managed the most popular ocean beachfront restaurant in the area. I was a daily playing beach volleyball player competing with some of Nor-Cal's best. On the court by 8:00–9:00 a.m., and trying to hold court. If you lost, you would have to sign up for the next opportunity to challenge the winners.

Every summer at Cowell's beach would be an all-division beach volleyball tournament. One summer, I decided to have the restaurant sponsor the tournament with T-shirts and prizes, and provide a fresh salmon, spuds, and salad dinner to all participants. I did this without the owners of the restaurant not fully behind the endeavor.

I built barbecue pits on the beach to cook the salmon and set up the table for salad and potatoes with condiments.

We were overwhelmed with the turnout! Almost five hundred meals—the owners of the restaurant were not really happy with me—$7 a head! It turned out fabulous! The restaurant owners were not happy with me even though the event generated business for "The Nest!"

WILT and his playing partner from UCLA, All-American, were the folks who came out to watch. My playing partner and I made it to the third round. If we would have won, we would have played WILT!

Still to this day, WILT made one of the greatest digs in volleyball I have ever seen. From the very back of the court, their opponents spiked a ball that looked like a sure winner. NO. WILT took one quick step and extended his arms with his gigantic flat-out hands and dug the ball out before the ball touched the sand and then miraculously passed the ball to his playing partner. WILT jumped up and pounded the ball that bounced fifteen feet high off the sand!

WILT was gracious and very entertaining to listen to when he held court! This tournament a few years later led to the world-famous "SANTA CRUZ OPEN!" Twenty years later, the owners who were not happy with me putting on this event eventually got permission from the city, Harbor Commission, to allow to have a complete restaurant barbecue setup on the beach, volleyball courts on the beach in front of the restaurant!

DONALD TRUMP JR.

My close friend from 1990–2017, BONNIE HAYDON of Denmark and resident of New York owned a top modeling agency in New York and through her late husband, he was a silent partner in "RAO'S."

Her daughter VANESSA was a beautiful model. The two of them attended a cocktail party in New York. As they both entered the function strikingly, businessman DONALD TRUMP noticed the stunning VANESSA from a distance entering the event. DONALD TRUMP b-lined directly to VANESSA and her mother BONNIE and introduced himself, not necessary, and chatted for some time in breaking the ice. DONALD TRUMP finally after the small talk conversation inquired about VANESSA'S dating availability, found out that she was single. He stated to VANESSA and BONNIE he would like to introduce his son, DONALD, Jr., as VANESSA's future husband! That started it all.

VOGAGER—FLYING NON-STOP AROUND THE GLOBE

JEANNA YEAGER and DICK RUTAN were the first pilots to fly non-stop around the globe in a small cramped ultra-light experimental plane RUTAN aeronautics designed. This had been attempted before with the challenge of no refueling or landings or stopping. Now can you imagine the discomfort they faced for eight days in a plane that they took turns in navigating. At one point, JEANNA YEAGER had to talk DICK RUTAN from not landing the plane and calling it quits due to his discomfort and anxiety. DICK RUTAN has created this image of toughness, and the strength of the team to prevail on their mission to circle the globe non-stop! This endeavor would be an aviation flying miracle! JEANNA YEAGER came across as a stern, reserved, introspective, quiet person. Let me tell you she was personable, fun, exciting, and full of energy compared to the reserved women that the press experienced. Full of "psst and vinegar!" What a strong woman! Our week together in Alabama as DICK RUTAN and YEAGER were judges in the MISS USA PAGEANT along with my friend ROSCOE TANNER. JEANNA YEAGER was like the ever-ready battery! She tackled every challenge athletically that she faced! I wish some of the athletes I worked with would have her tenacity to never back down from a challenge and compete with every obstacle! One of my favorite people!

MISS USA PAGEANT, SELMA, ALABAMA

I was introduced to BONNIE HAYDON as a guest of ROSCOE TANNER during the MISS USA pageant in Selma, Alabama. The pageant had seven celebrity judges for the pageant. DICK RUTAN and JEANNA YEAGER were pilots who flew the VOYAGER around the globe without stopping DEBBIE REYNOLDS, RICHARD ANDERSON, and others.

As a judge, you were monitored and provided security when you ventured out of your accommodations. The guests of the judges were also provided security. We realized very quickly that they took the MISS USA contest seriously. It was serious when I went to the bathroom, and security would not allow anyone into the bathroom when I was there. In the past, family members of contestants would approach judges and even their guests to influence the outcome of various stages of the pageant.

I finally could relate to what private security for individuals was all about.

This was big business that some of the contestants who had ribs removed, feet sculped for heels, and the usual stuff, breast augmentation and liposuction.

DICK CLARK shared with ROSCOE TANNER (judge) this scenario. At the start of the week, fifty-one contestants will do anything for you and love you during the interview process, evening gown and bathing suit segment (they have now changed the format), then the first cut.

Eleven contestants hate you, and forty still will say or do anything for you during the next interview segment. On the second cut, thirty will hate you. Additionally, family members are all on board not liking you as well. Then ten will say or do anything for you in the third stage of the interview segment. Then on the third cut, five will hate you, then five will still do anything for you. Then on the fourth cut on the stage after interview segment, three will hate you. Then the two finalists, for all the marbles, then one will hate you. And the winner won't give a damn!

COLONEL SANDERS AND "KENTUCKY FRIED CHICKEN"

My buddy and I were traveling and relocating to Charleston, South Carolina, to consult and open a restaurant.

My buddy had a family friend who was in the horse business in Shelbyville, Kentucky. They raised and trained equestrian horses, racing horses, and even owned and published the world's top horse magazine.

As we arrived on the grounds at sunset, it was September and the "lightning bugs" were on full display. The yearling's horses were about twenty and were out of the barn enjoying the cool evening sunset.

I decided to jump out of the car and introduce myself to these beautiful animals. It was a rush to say the least running with horses and "lightning bugs" on this beautiful estate.

The collective value of these horses was over hundreds of millions of dollars.

A few of the horses got attached to me. Our guest house was adjacent to the barn of the yearlings. Each morning, the horses would come to the windows to investigate and greet whoever turned on the morning light.

I was sitting on the crown reading the newspaper with the bathroom window open, and all of a sudden, I was drenched with water. The horses came to the window when they saw the light come on in the bathroom. They were drooling on me with slobber! I jumped unexpectedly to see the three horses heads in the window who were startled and bumped their heads on the window frame. I couldn't stop laughing!

That evening, we were invited to dinner at COLONEL SANDER'S home for dinner. Our hosts said, "Don't ask what you are being served because it is southern hospitality." The restaurant was their home with living quarters on the second floor.

I learned he was given the title COLONEL as an honorary honor which he kept for his lifetime.

He originally owned and operated a gas station. Executives were visiting his gas station and were concerned with a local competitor had placed marketing billboards around "COLONEL'S" gas station.

One of the executives had a confrontation with the competing business owner and violence ensued. Out of self-defense, the "COLONEL" shot and killed his business competitor after he had shot and killed one of the executives. The "COLONEL" was vindicated when charges were dismissed "in self-defense."

The "COLONEL" opened up "THE COLONEL'S LADY (CLAUDIA) DINNER HOUSE" named after his wife CLAUDIA. This naming was a legal issue where "COLONEL SANDER'S" was awarded one million dollars in a lawsuit to change its name to be able to be in business.

We had a fabulous dinner engaging in southern cooking traditions that weren't offered in what we know as "KFC." The highlight of the evening was the "COLONEL" visiting our table with an animated conversation recognizing our hosts. He used profanity mild at our table in our conversation. He was not in good health, but I enjoyed the iconic moment. Unfortunately, he passed a few years later, I never forgot that evening.

His home and restaurant burnt down in 1999.

"KING KONG" AND "WEST SIDE STORY"

One of my all-time memories of two of "HOLLYWOOD'S" most memorable movies.

My father took me to a showing of the 1933 classic *King Kong* at the Varsity Theater in Palo Alto, California, in the late '50s, when I was eight years old. It was ranked as the fourth greatest horror film of all time, and the forty-sixth greatest film of all time.

Everyone knows how the original movie ends with the ROBERT ARMSTRONG character "CARL DENHAM" who captured and brought "KING KONG" to NEW YORK from "KONG ISLAND."

CARL DENHAM stood above "KING KONG" lying at the street below at "THE EMPIRE STATE" building and declared, "It was beauty that killed the beast." Diverting his death from being shot down to the beauty of FAY WRAY (ANN DARROW).

My father directed the movie theater usher (gave him a few bucks) to come to our seats and escort me out of the theater before "KONG's" eventual demise. My father thought the ending would be too traumatic for a young child.

It took me years to finally see the ending.

Throughout the upcoming years, there were numerous remakes of the historic King Kong. My father passed in December 2005, and the great director PETER JACKSON (LORD of the RINGS, Trilogy) released King Kong. That week, I went to the opening of *King Kong*, and out of respect for "KING KONG" and my father, I left the theater before the ending. I left on a happy note when "KING KONG" was playfully in Central Park sliding in the snow.

A similar story, but this is with *West Side Story* and my mother.

My mother decided to take my sister and I by train to Philadelphia for a shopping adventure and to see a movie matinee of *West Side Story*. Mom and Dad had seen the play on Broadway and they enjoyed the production. The year was 1961, and we were very young.

My mother also took the same direction as my father in telling and directing the movie usher to seek us out and for us to sit in the lobby until the movie was concluded. (Under supervision.)

So it took years to finally absorb the totality of the movie and its messages of love, life, and culture.

Years later, I did a magazine shoot on health, etc., that had "NATALIE WOOD" former husband "ROBERT WAGNER" on the cover who discovered her body from a mysterious drowning off the Catalina Islands from his boat.

THE FAMED HEARST ESTATE, BEVERLY HILLS

One of my first clients was the body double for JACQUELIN BISSET for the movie called *The Deep* and starring NICK NOTTLE and RAY SCHROEDER.

The opening scene with the wet T-shirt sequence of JACQUELIN BISSET emerging from the water to the dive boat is one of HOLLYWOOD'S most iconic scenes.

The body double was married to BILL DANIELS, owner of PRIME TICKET and a heavy hitter with the HOLLYWOOD crowd. He was a successful businessman involved with his signature from SPORTS to HOLLYWOOD.

My client asked me if I would like to attend a private birthday bash for GREG DAVIES'S thirtieth birthday party. I said "sure!"

My invitation arrived via limousine at my business. The invitation was sealed in a box covered with feathers from exotic birds and delivered by a gentleman in a tuxedo.

The "Birthday Bash" was to be held at his father's residence, "WILLIAM RANDOLPH HEARST AND MARION DAVIES" mansion in Beverly Hills.

When we arrived, we were greeted at the first checkpoint for identification and social security number. Then proceeded to the second checkpoint for party name tags and gift bags.

The pool had an active volcano in the middle and the surrounding area had an island theme. There was everything imaginable around the pool. After being served a drink of your choice, hors d'oeuvres were plentiful that represented various island cultures throughout the world. I had my astrological star chart prepared, palms read, and various other types of readings.

The estate was used in the movies *The Godfather* and *The Bodyguard* and has played host to politicians, business magnates, and celebrities, and even in 1953, JACQUELINE and JOHN F. KENNEDY spent their honeymoon on the three-and-a-half romantic acre spread.

MARVIN DAVIS, CHAIRMAN OF UNIVERSAL and homeowner at the time, built a flowing river in the circus tent area for his son's thirtieth birthday.

The food was flown in from various parts of the world and was outstanding! In my estimation, it probably cost around five million for his son's birthday.

The twenty-nine-thousand-square-foot main house features twenty-two-foot hand-painted ceilings, a two-story paneled library, two screening rooms, and a bar salvaged from HUGH HEFNER'S nightclub.

The billiards rooms are original floors and stone moved down from HEARST'S former home HEARST CASTLE in San Simeon.

The mansion is shaped like an *H* and holds eight bedrooms and extends to various patios and balconies.

The vintage lampposts light manicured gardens outside, and the grounds feature fountains, loggias, lawns, terraces, a tennis court, and a breathtaking pool. The bathroom was only challenged by SINATRAS!

A night to remember!

STANLEY KRAMER, DIRECTOR, *RPM!*

I was planning to go skiing during Christmas break in Squaw Valley with my high school buddies.

I got a call from my uncle who asked me what did I have planned during my upcoming holidays. I shared with him, "I was heading to Lake Tahoe to go skiing."

He asked me if I would like to be an extra in a Hollywood movie production at my parent's alma mater. He shared that I could make up to one thousand plus for a week to ten days.

I'm in high school, in great shape, just finished football and lacrosse season playing basketball on the team, and one thousand dollars is a lot for a high school kid in 1970.

I had no idea what to expect when I arrived to check in on the set. I had a connection because my uncle and his best friend BILL HICKMAN were friends of the director.

RPM was the name of the movie. The movie's theme was current at the time regarding the political unrest on campuses during the Vietnam War. The UNIVERSITY of PACIFIC campus was the setting for the movie.

I was an extra for 1,000! Except when my uncle and BILL HICKMAN arranged for me to be a riot policeman in full riot gear! There were a hundred of us in full policemen uniforms, riot helmets, face masks, batons, and shields, and all hundreds of us looked like real riot controllers.

The first day at 8:00 a.m., all one hundred of us, "THE RIOT POLICEMEN." were instructed that the additional nine hundred extras would be storming us from all directions (all of them looked like hippies from that era, 1969) and they would take their anger upon us!

The horn blew at about 11:00 a.m. for "action" and within minutes, our lines were broken by the acting VIETNAM college movie protesters. The age of the movie extra protesters looked older to me than 1969 college students.

In the movie, extra college movie protesters took their acting roles a little too seriously! Four football-sized guys grabbed my arms and legs and used me as a battering ram against a tree! I was laughing at these guys taking their roles a little too seriously and trying to inflict bodily harm upon me. Thank god my helmet was secure! I could not stop laughing as they tried to inflict pain upon me as I shouted out, "This is a movie!" I was happy I was in GREAT athletic shape for this type of punishment!

I was happy when the bullhorn director said, "CUT!"

The following morning, on the set, I was dressed for another shoot in my "riot policeman's uniform," with a new helmet. The director called out my badge number to report to the director's area.

They inquired and showed audio of me laughing and "telling the rioters they were taking an acting job too seriously!" "We are filming a major motion picture and you have caused us to reshoot this scene again. It is very expensive for us!"

The director inquired about my name and how did I get into this movie.

I told him who I was, my uncle's name, and our friend BILL HICKMAN!

He started laughing and said, "That figures!" He instructed the staff to have me sit in the proximity of the stars and "be prepared when we insert you to the scenes." All of a sudden, I became one of the top policemen extras.

For the next week, I rubbed elbows with the stars of the movie: ANTHONY QUINN, ANN MARGARET, PAUL WINFIELD, and GARY LOCKWOOD.

GARY LOCKWOOD recently finished shooting the masterpiece ARTHUR C. CLARK'S *2001: A Space Odyssey* directed by STANLEY KUBRICK. GARY took me under his wing and showed me how to pitch quarters. He never showed remorse for taking money off a high school student.

The director of *RPM*, STANLEY KRAMER produced such HOLLYWOOD masterpieces as *High Noon, Ship of Fools, Judgement at Nuremberg, On the Beach, Wild Ones, Caine Mutiny, It's a Mad, Mad, Mad World, The Defiant Ones,* and *Guess Who's Coming to Dinner*—a "HALL OF FAME MOTION PICTURE RESUME" including me in *RPM*!

In conversation with "ANTHONY QUINN" and "ANN MARGRET," they both said basically the same thing the *RPM* was not one of their most memorable roles, but the money was good!

SHERWOOD COUNTRY CLUB

"SHARK SHOOTOUT"

The stars were aligned for me to have the opportunity to be employed, assist, and consult for a new exclusive country club in THOUSAND OAKS, CALIFORNIA.

A community for the rich and famous billionaire DAVID MURDOCK'S oak studied SHERWOOD COUNTRY CLUB. He invested more than $200 million to build the best new golf course an hour from downtown LOS ANGELES.

The property that DAVID MURDOCK purchased was used as "SHERWOOD FOREST" in the ROBIN HOOD movies with ERROL FLYNN and a few other HOLLYWOOD productions.

DAVID MURDOCK is the owner of DOLE FOOD CO., which includes DOLE PINEAPPLE, and previously owned 80 percent of the Island of LANAI, which he recently sold to LARRY ELLISON of ORACLE.

MURDOCK also owns Arabian Horses and a beautiful ranch across the street from SHERWOOD COUNTRY CLUB.

The golf field for the GREG NORMAN "SHARK SHOOTOUT" consisted of CURTIS STRANGE, MARK O'MEARA, TOM WEISKOPF, LANNY WADKINS, ANDY BEAN, BERNARD LANGER, JOHN MAHAFFEY, RAY FLOYD, GREG NORMAN (host), JACK NICKLAUS, ARNOLD PALMER, HALE IRWIN, CURTIS STRANGE, FRED COUPLES, PETER JACOBSON, IAN

BAKER FINCH, BEN CRENSHAW, WAYNE LEVI, ANDY BEAN, BRUCE LIETZKE, GIL MORGAN.

The announcer starter was SHERWOOD'S COUNTRY HEAD TENNIS professional ROSCOE TANNER. ROSCOE really embraced his position, he wore a tie and jacket, and thoroughly enjoyed introducing the players.

After a practice round, some of the players sat at our table for lunch. The group included FRED COUPLES, HALE IRWIN, PETER JACOBSON, IAN BAKER FINCH, "TOURNAMENT HOST" GREG NORMAN, ARNOLD PALMER, ROSCOE TANNER, and myself.

Some of the entertaining conversation during lunch was HALE IRWIN trying to justify the COLORADO BUFFALO college football team winning a football game by the officials forgetting what down it was.

HALE IRWIN was a former football player with the COLORADO BUFFALO football team (There are not too many PGA Tour players with a college football background).

HALE IRWIN leads the PGA CHAMPIONS TOUR with forty-five victories. BERNARD LANGER has forty-three, and he is sixty-four! LANGER has fifteen straight years with a victory on the PGA CHAMPIONS TOUR.

Back to the BUFFALOS and HALE IRWIN. PETER JACOBSON was giving IRWIN some friendly banter. Questioning the coach's integrity, etc., and JACOBSON said, "The extra down led to BUFFALO tarnished victory."

I came to the conclusion tuning in it was IRWIN'S way or NO one else's.

Then I had an interesting conversation with FRED COUPLES privately. We knew each other since he resided at MISSION HILLS COUNTRY CLUB, and I was a trainer of numerous players at MISSION HILLS, COUNTRY CLUB.

I worked with a good friend of his, GEORGE BRETT of KANSAS CITY ROYALS, and future BASEBALL HALL OF FAMER.

Recently, I was having some luck with some caddying and training PGA TOUR players. I won and tied in HOWARD COSELL ALL-AMERICAN CHAMPIONSHIP at MORNINGSIDE COUNTRY CLUB, RANCHO MIRAGE. FRED also played in the event, and we chatted throughout the day when our paths crossed during the round.

I got into a serious chat about the big "three" of his golf game. In all competitive sports, it is mental/emotional/physical characteristics of sport.

I had watched his most recent PGA tournament and down the stretch, in contention, he made some mental/emotional errors to not getting into the winner's circle.

I shared with him my observations and told him to become a champion he needed to address this!

Sure enough, the following year in '92, he was in contention on the back nine at the MASTERS. (The best-televised tournament in sports used to be only two minutes of commercials per hour). FRED hit the most memorable shot of his career. On #12 his approach shot hit the shaved bank, divine intervention occurred, and the ball stayed up where 99.9% of all shots roll back into the water. He went on to win the "GREEN JACKET!"

Anyway, back to lunch.

During lunch, DAVID MURDOCK approached the table and asked to speak with "TOURNAMENT HOST" GREG NORMAN.

GREG NORMAN got up from his chair and stood directly behind me with DAVID MURDOCK, an earshot for me to hear their conversation while the rest of the table kept busy in conversation.

DAVID MURDOCK reminded GREG NORMAN about the barbecue dinner he was having at his ranch later in the evening. An evening only for players, their wives, and special guests including the new "DIRECTOR of TRAINING," "MOIS!"

As I eased into their conversation (I was NOT obvious) so DAVID MURDOCK said to GREG NORMAN, "He would like GREG to put on an apron and be the barbecue cook?"

GREG NORMAN said sternly NO!

DAVID MURDOCK replied, "Oh yes, you are!"

GREG NORMAN answered again, "No I'm not!"

At this time, a little premature verbal firework started only within earshot of my acute perfect hearing!

DAVID MURDOCK reminded GREG NORMAN that he "had flown in AUSTRALIAN LOBSTER, RIBS, and other specialties for the tournament players and guests for the dinner at his ranch."

DAVID MURDOCK reminded GREG NORMAN, "He was paying him a half-million dollars ($ 500,000.00) to host this tournament in his name, and to provide global marketing of his brand."

GREG NORMAN insisted that he was the star for the tournament, and DAVID MURDOCK could provide the staff to cook.

So it was a wait-and-see. I told ROSCOE (I was his house guest) what was discussed, and he was anxious to see who would be manning the barbecue.

I had the opportunity to be in a small group "HALL of FAME" golfers for the first dinner at DAVID MURDOCK'S ranch during the GREG NORMAN "SHARK SHOOTOUT," and was looking forward to the dinner. And made a friendly handshake bet with ROSCOE TANNER NORMAN would be behind the grill!

ROSCOE, wife CHARLOTTE, and I arrived. We parked where everyone else had parked.

I noticed BERNARD LANGER walking alongside me. I said, "Good evening, great ranch!" BERNARD LANGER said, "It's beautiful," then I said, "I caddied in a group with you at RIVIERA COUNTRY CLUB, PALISADES, CALIFORNIA, caddying for GARY HALLBERG."

"You had one of the greatest pars I have ever witnessed on hole # 16, par 3. You hit your iron tee shot in the worst sand trap for a difficult up and down for a par, and tough pin placement. Your second shot from the trap skied the green and settled in the other trap across the green. You were looking at double bogie if you were lucky! So you, BERNARD, settled in a swung hard and holed the shot for an unbelievable up and down par!"

He laughed. "That's why I practice." And we changed the subject.

ROSCOE, CHARLOTTE, and I were excited to see what transpired in the earlier conversation by DAVID MURDOCK with GREG NORMAN if he was going behind the pit cooking ribs, etc.

Sure enough, GREG NORMAN was cooking ribs, burgers, and chicken, and he was enjoying it. He was personable, laughing, and seemed to be enjoying himself. MURDOCH was pleased!

So the three of us sat directly in front of the barbecue. There were only about forty of us at the festivities.

At our table were tournament host GREG NORMAN, PETER JACOBSON, ARNOLD PALMER, ROSCOE, and CHARLOTTE TANNER, LANNY WADKINS, IAN BAKER FINCH, FRED COUPLES, and Mois.

PETER JACOBSON broke out singing, "SHE DRIVES ME CRAZY," FINE YOUNG CANNIBALS hit. I started to sing, and ROSCOE said, "My man can hit the notes." I have sung with some of the best!

I got up from the table to pursue attacking the dessert table. I saw BARBARA NICKLAUS and said hi! We introduced ourselves.

I have learned throughout the years to engage in small talk and normal conversation, and be open to talk about everything.

About ten minutes into chatting, SIR JACK NICKLAUS the GOAT (the GREATEST OF ALL TIME) joined us. Our conversation quickly went to tennis and WIMBLEDON.

MR. NICKLAUS would invite players to his home and practice on his grass courts growing different turf for his various worldwide projects, put tennis posts in, and would let tour tennis players prepare for the grass-court season. He plays tennis, but not as much anymore.

I had to pinch myself for an evening under the stars and with golf stars and legends.

The next morning, I called my father and shared with him my evening.

The following week was Thanksgiving week and the SKIN'S GAME at PGA WEST, LA QUINTA. My parents were homeowners.

My mother always volunteered and oversaw the scorer's volunteers.

My mother had shared my stories from the previous week at the "SHARK SHOOTOUT," and myself rubbing elbows with everyone.

My mother and her friends and fellow club members saw BARBARA NICKLAUS approaching from a distance. My mother's fellow volunteers and members egged her on to go introduce herself.

As my mother approached BARBARA NICKLAUS, my mother was hoping I didn't fill her head with lots of BS and wouldn't embarrass her when she introduced herself.

My mother introduced herself, with her fellow members in tow, and said, "My tennis son met you last week at the SHARK SHOOTOUT at SHERWOOD COUNTRY CLUB?" Before my mother could mention her last name, BARBARA NICKLAUS said, "You're RANDY'S mother? What a nice young man. I enjoyed our time chatting."

Mom's fellow volunteers and club members were impressed! Most importantly, my mother was relieved! Take a moment and think about how many people BARBARA NICKLAUS meets?

The next day was THANKSGIVING. My family had reservations at the PGA WEST CLUBHOUSE, main dining room.

My father saw CURTIS STRANGE sitting at a nearby table. I told him I met and chatted with him at the "SHARK SHOOTOUT" as well.

Pops said, "I would like to meet him." And sure enough, I approached the table, said hi, and introduced my dad, and CURTIS introduced us to his family. I told him, "My parents were homeowners." CURTIS STRANGE was very nice and cordial.

A memorable two weeks with the future "HALL OF FAME" golfers!

CADDYING—PGA TOUR, LPGA TOUR, ETC.

It all started for me when I was a very young man. Eleven years old!

My mother who was a terrific golfer was playing as an amateur in a field that had professional women players at TURF VALLEY COUNTRY CLUB in MARYLAND.

At the time, there really wasn't a women's tour. Some of the participants were CAROL MANN, SANDRA PALMER, and the founders of the LPGA TOUR.

I had a push cart from my mother to make it easy for me to get around the course.

So on the course, I was pulling this old ancient cart to today's standards. On the twelfth hole, I gave my mother her three-wood and ventured up the fairway to meet her for her second shot.

A little dogleg to the left, and I waited for her.

Her t-shot hit the bag and myself! Welcome to the big leagues!

LPGA QUALIFYING SCHOOL

NATALIE GILBUS, STACY LEWIS, MICHELLE WIE, JENNY CHUASIRAORN, SUN HE LEE (SUNNY LEE), PAULA CREAMER, YOUNG A YANG, AMANDA BLOOMQUEST, etc.

I got a call from an agent about a KOREAN young lady who was KOREA'S top female golfer and recognized as one of the sexiest KOREAN athletes.

SUN HE LEE had attempted to qualify for the LPGA numerous times without much success.

So anyway, I told the agent that if I wasn't successful getting SUN HE LEE through the first stage, that would enable her to qualify for the final stage of LPGA tour stage she would not have to pay me! A WIN-WIN!

Well, we comfortably qualified during the first stage at MISSION HILLS COUNTRY CLUB. I have played the two qualifying courses numerous times due to working with numerous tennis players at the club.

They play the ARNOLD PALMER COURSE one of the first two days and the DINAH SHORE TOURNAMENT COURSE for three days if they make the cut after the first two rounds.

Remember we play at the end of summer when the temperatures exceed 100+ degrees. The course is so different than when the first major is played, and players would have to make numerous adjustments.

The final five holes on the ARNOLD PALMER course are really challenging especially having to make the cut!

SUN HE LEE closed with birdie, birdie, par, par, birdie.

Before we met and played practice rounds, I went to the local library and picked up a book on KOREAN language. So I worked on phrases to communicate to SUN HE LEE that she would understand.

I did this because I noticed in our practice rounds with AMERICAN players and their caddies would make notations in their yardage books with what I was telling SUN HE LEE about directional shot selection, club selection, and green approach positioning off the tee box, fairway, etc. I knew this course better than most people.

Remember there are ONLY so many spots available to move forward to the finals in DAYTONA, FLORIDA. My approach worked great with my player and myself. I attached my phrases to my yardage books. The opposition asked me if I spoke KOREAN, and I said YES!

Anyway, we made the finals comfortably and prepared to go to DAYTONA, FLORIDA, to play the LPGA championships courses to try to qualify for attaining the LPGA card.

Our practice rounds to prepare were interesting. We played every practice round with rising star NATALIE GULBIS of SACRAMENTO, CALIFORNIA.

NATALIE GULBIS was a teenage prodigy who was playing her first professional tournaments as a teenager. NATALIE made a splash when she finally got to the big leagues with her smile, appeal, and the big game!

SUN HE LEE and I walked the course every practice round with NATALIE, and her father rode in a golf cart, strategically from afar. We had a great time practicing and preparing for qualifying.

Our first few days were entertaining! When SUN HE LEE sank a putt for birdie or par, she would turn and wave her hand to a non-existent crowd preparing herself for being on the LPGA tour with the crowds.

One day in qualifying, it rained really hard for a few delays, three on-course delays; and the course had snakes! YES, snakes everywhere on fairways, hanging from trees, etc. It was really bizarre seeing six-to-eight-foot snakes scoring across fairways, greens, and sand traps and it was a six-and-a-half-hour round to complete.

Unknown to me, SUN HE LEE had her boyfriend arrive the night before Q-school started for the tourney week. During such an intense week of securing your card! I told him diplomatically to take a back seat during the week and NOT interfere with a goal that has been unattainable.

The final round was challenging with the psychological challenges, the course setup, the delays due to weather, and the players in our group.

SUN HE LEE played a solid back nine and played even par. After the final putt on eighteenth hole, she felt she qualified to secure her LPGA card for the upcoming year. The KOREAN press overwhelmed her as she reported her score to the scorer's tent off the green. There were still players finishing on the front nine to take into consideration. These players would have to shoot low numbers since they started well behind us.

SUN HE LEE and I walked to the car to leave and go back to the hotel. I intervened and said, "I am going up to the scorer's tournament main desk at the clubhouse, it's NOT over until all participants have submitted their scores."

Sure enough, there were nine players who tied us! Now we were in a 4-hole playoff with nine players for four spots. Imagine having to get her head ready to go play into a playoff.

Three groups in threesomes. We were in the last group, advantageous to know where we stood. Some of the players' friends would give us the results of the groups ahead (we trusted them, which made me uncomfortable) of us to know exactly where we stood to qualify.

There was one spot available as we stood in the fairway at eighteen. The scenario was a player in our group had to hole her approach, unlikely, and the other players just had to get up and down to knock us out. The player nuked her shot over the green in a very difficult position to get "up and down" a bogie at best. I insisted to my player "center of the green" two putts for a par! Sure enough, the player over the green couldn't get up and down, and SUN HE LEE secured her card! The KOREAN press once again went nuts! SUN HE LEE was a big star in KOREA, 5'11" great looking, and sexy!

A month later, SUN HE LEE rented a house at PGA WEST where I lived so I could assist her in getting ready for the LPGA tour. I would arrange SUN HE LEE to play practice rounds with some of my professionals or top amateur players.

One of my "Cafe" regulars, a young wealthy golfer who recently sold his "SOFTWARE" company for millions lived at one of the USA'S top private exclusive clubs, THE VINTAGE in INDIAN WELLS.

I asked him, "That I had a few top players who would like the opportunity to play THE VINTAGE if the opportunity arises?" I shared, "I had two women and two mini-school male players." So he arranged for them to play as a fivesome at THE VINTAGE.

The host hit it off with SUN HE LEE! He fell head over heels with her! His girlfriend, the former MISS TEXAS, was dumped! She called me and asked me what had transpired and if I knew about SUN HE LEE?

I had no clue! MISS TEXAS even arrived from D.C. a few days later to investigate. I shared with her, "I arranged ONLY a golf group to play!"

Anyway, the VINTAGE member fell in love with her! And he insisted that he would fly her on his private jet to every tournament for the upcoming LPGA TOUR. Not too many rookies get those types of parts, etc. She embraced it!

He wanted her to quit and would take care of her financially!

SUN HE LEE played in twenty-four LPGA TOUR events and SUN HE LEE NEVER made a cut! NEVER! This is the first time an LPGA golfer in LPGA TOUR history to accomplish that feat!

SUN HE LEE resorted to playing member women's club championships, members, guests, etc., and would shoot midsixties consistency. She dominated! SUN HE LEE even changed her name to SUNNY LEE to sound more AMERICAN. The two of them are living happily together at THE VINTAGE CLUB and in TEXAS.

I became a marked man by LPGA for my honest observations. In time, I looked like a genius!

SUN HE LEE was one of a few KOREAN golfers I successfully worked with. In time, AMERICAN players were not happy that I successfully got KOREAN players their LPGA cards!

One of the most memorable players that I helped for only two rounds in LPGA qualifying school was the wonderful JENNY CHUSSIRAPORN of DUKE UNIVERSITY.

JENNY was a roommate of tennis player VANESSA WEBB at DUKE UNIVERSITY who I worked with, and VANESSA WEBB not only WON NCAA singles CHAMPIONSHIP, but additionally, she won ACADEMIC first TEAM ALL-AMERICAN! (Read about her in the tennis section.)

I was contacted by VANESSA if I could help her roommate to QUALIFY for the LPGA TOUR at MISSION HILLS COUNTRY CLUB.

Unfortunately, I had a prior engagement to attend a wedding of one of my former pupils in SEATTLE.

I told her I could work the first two rounds. JENNY played solidly and was in a comfortable position to qualify for the final.

One of the biggest mistakes I made as a caddie was NOT to finish the job I had started. I regret it to this day. I felt that the two of us could have changed the LPGA forever.

To refresh your memory, JENNY had one of the most improbable finishes in U.S. OPEN major history. JENNY sank a fifty-plus putt on the final hole to force an 18-hole playoff the following day.

It came down to the final hole, and the USGA made a historic ruling blunder! USGA took the trophy out of JENNY'S hands. SER RI PAK got a break on an errant shot. They and the USGA bent the rules for looking for a lost ball. For an extra five minutes, JENNY patiently waited, and waited, and waited, and missed a putt to send the U.S. WOMENS to additional holes.

I felt it was all about $$$ to bring in the KOREAN audience, but it started a BOOM of KOREAN golf! A huge travesty.

Throughout the next few years, I had a direct line to assist KOREAN players in Q-school. Some AMERICAN players were NOT happy with me assisting KOREAN players to their success on the tour! The LPGA is dominated by KOREAN players.

Then came an AMERICAN KOREAN (descent) from SO-CAL.

We played in 110+ heat for four days. On the second day, two groups playing in front of us dropped some players due to the heat because of this, it opened numerous holes in front of us. The tour official put us on the clock. We basically put on our jets and played lights out. And on top of this, the other caddies in our group didn't do SHIT!

My gal was exhausted due to physical or lack of physical conditioning. After our final round, where she qualified for the finals while negotiating in the victory meal, I made my hiring an afterthought, her team wasn't right in the head! She didn't get through the next stage.

I did not enjoy the one Q-school where I was contacted by an agent to see if I was available to work with a former USC player.

From the first day when asked to join a prayer family group, you need all the help you can muster and nothing better than the big guy overlooking your game. Unfortunately, divine intervention only can take you so far, because eventually, your feet have to be grounded.

I DO NOT take responsibility of the players shots that is why we practice so you execute what you practice. You have to go from the range to the course!

I have NEVER quit or walked off the course, but I had enough of her not being able to hit the shot required at this level.

We parted ways after the tenth hole. I just kept my mouth shut, pulled flags, raked traps, and drove the cart.

I was professional, got paid 75% of my salary, and she still had the final round! She flat out, told me she would perform better with someone else, so she was five over par on the final day. The worst round by four strokes when I looped for her—USC—UNIVERSITY OF SPOILED CHILDREN!

STACY LEWIS competed in Q-school at MISSION HILLS.

I remember first seeing her carrying her own bag to the range, then carrying it to the short game area, and doing everything on her own. You just don't see that much!

AMANDA BLOOMQUEST had the potential she never tapped into! Going from a college star to the tour is difficult! Too deep of talented players! I noticed watching her from afar that the qualifying would be a rude awakening!

MICHELLE WIE was also at MISSION HILLS for qualifying. I was amassed by her height and physical presence. She was surrounded by the press anticipating the rise of a future star. She had a disappointing career when considering how many promises she had.

PAULA CREAMER is another rising star!

I worked with a gal who played her collegiate golf at VANDERBILT UNIVERSITY. Talented, competitive, smart, and good-looking!

We played our first two rounds with PAULA on the DINAH SHORE TOURNAMENT COURSE at MISSION HILLS. Each player and caddy were provided a cart due to the heat. The rules only one person from your team could ride while the other walked.

On our first day competing, we rotated who would ride, and the other walked. My gal was a bit overwhelmed playing with one of the hottest upcoming stars on the future tour. My gal got into the mindset that she was playing match play with CREAMER and total disregard for the third player in our group.

PAULA'S caddy was the caddy who was with her for a number of years. He would get down to the putting level on the green like he was ready to do a push-up. He was a bit cocky! They felt they could intimate us!

After an over par *round*, we went up to the clubhouse for lunch, and I discussed a different strategy for the following day on THE OLD COURSE.

I made my gal walk to pace herself! Only pay attention and have blinders on to focus on OUR game and approach. Ride in the cart when we had a long distance between green and t-box, or only in a situation, I suggested to ride! Our approach worked GREAT! -3 on the old course and when we finished. We had thumped our opponent PAULA CREAMER! Their team was in disarray.

Unfortunately, after four rounds, and a ten-foot birdie, she missed advancing to the finals by one stroke. In her next stage, she made the finals. I thoroughly enjoyed working with her and helping her elevate her game. Confidence can go a long way!

USC/JIM EMPEY/CHRIS ZAMBRI

JIM EMPEY was the golf coach at the UNIVERSITY OF SOUTHERN CALIFORNIA.

His parents were both on the teaching staff as professors at the UNIVERSITY.

I met JIM when I was caddying when he played in the group with one of my players. He inquired about what I was doing in the golf world.

He asked me if I would be interested to come and speak to his team at USC and share what I was doing to improve his golf game. The entire men's team, a few of the women's players from the USC women's team, and a few others joined the afternoon.

I brought two of my players who were just starting to go to the next level in professional golf.

A few of the USC team members, both men and women, pursued taking their game to the next level.

I ran into one of the stars from the team at a NIKE PGA TOUR event in SOUTH DAKOTA. He had a talent but was too analytical for the game. He eventually became the head golf coach at the UNIVERSITY of SOUTHERN CALIFORNIA.

JIM EMPEY was one of the most enjoyable guys to be around. He returned to his hometown of BOISE, IDAHO, where he and his wife (a successful lawyer in BOISE) live to this day. He recently qualified for THE SENIOR PGA CHAMPIONSHIP, and a great feat to make the field. To days of '80s!

JIM is still involved with the BOISE OPEN on the PGA Tour.

PGA Q-SCHOOL

ROBIN FREEMAN, ROBERT GAMEZ

The winningest QUALIFYING SCHOOL money leader participant was ROBIN FREEMAN of PALM DESERT, CALIFORNIA.

Normally, if you win what is considered the most difficult, and challenging event in sports, PGA QUALIFYING SCHOOL, most golfers usually don't return to qualifying school, but ROBIN did. Not only did he return to Q-school again, but WON the QUALIFYING school again! Twice in a five-year period! Never done before until the past few years!

ROBIN and I had some success on the tour. We won twice and finished second on the NIKE TOUR money list!

At the TOUR CHAMPIONSHIP in ALABAMA, ROBIN only had to finish in the top six to win the TOUR money CHAMPIONSHIP. The benefit of winning the TOUR money title is you write your own ticket for tournaments for the following year except for the majors.

On the fifteenth hole, we were informed by television media that we were in second place and in a position to win the TOUR MONEY TITLE.

ROBIN turned to me and said, "I don't want to win the tour money title because it's for losers." I looked at him in disbelief and puzzlement and started to fire off names of all the PGA TOUR players who went on to be successful in advancing from the minor tour.

Our group finished ahead of players who were still on the course who also had a chance to win the TOUR MONEY TITLE.

As we were eating lunch, ROBIN was being besieged by agents, club manufacturers, and everyone else. ROBIN was watching the broadcast and was seeing if anyone could knock us off the money title.

Then he said to me, "I really want to win the money title." A little late for that. We had complete control of golf course earlier!

ROBIN is one of three sons who all played professional golf in some capacity or another.

JEFF, the younger brother, played on NIKE TOUR and got into the field at some PGA TOUR events. The youngest of the FREEMAN boys took the path to be a PGA TOUR professional and become a club and director and head golf professional at numerous COACHELLA COUNTRY CLUBS.

ROBIN is a teaching professional in the COACHELLA VALLEY, director of Golf Instruction at Tahquitz Golf Resort, and works with numerous top professional prospects.

I have not spoken to him for a few years. We both had divorces!

ROBERT GAMEZ

I got together when he moved to the desert to work on his game.

He contacted me after seeing me on the golf channel and read some media print about my program.

ROBERT GAMEZ came to the desert to play in BOB HOPE GOLF TOURNAMENT. We had spent some time on the course to get to know each other.

He had not been playing well!

He rented a home at the CITRUS COUNTRY CLUB in LA QUINTA with his future wife.

I would come over and we would walk out onto the golf course and hit some shots. One of the most important characteristics of golf is your confidence.

ROBERT had an explosive introduction to the PGA TOUR. He won his first PGA Professional Tournament. That victory secures his card, exempt for two years, and makes you financially secure.

Then a few weeks later, he was playing ARNOLD PALMERS HONDA CLASSIC and came to the final hole. GAMEZ needed his fairway shot to have a chance to win, and sure enough, he slams dunked a shot from the fairway to beat GREG NORMAN and the rest of the field.

I was home at PGA WEST watching and listening to the tournament and the crowd roaring, and I finally heard from the announcers that GAMEZ was threatening to break sixty. He had to shoot two under on the final holes!

Living on the course, I could hear the crowd roaring for the opportunity to see a player break sixty! He finished strong and shot a sixty-one!

My mother was a volunteer and head scorer and recorded DAVID DUVAL'S fifty-nine on the final SUNDAY.

So the following day, ROBERT GAMEZ and his future wife came in for breakfast. The "Cafe" was packed, and I took a moment to inform the guests who ROBERT GAMEZ was and what he accomplished the previous day shooting a sixty-one. The guests gave him a standing ovation, cheered, and ROBERT was embarrassed and moved by the acknowledgment. It was really cool!

Later in the year, ROBERT approached me about caddying in the second stage of qualifying for the PGA TOUR. The stage was locally at a good golf track that I was familiar with.

So we spent time together playing the course and developing a strategy for our play. I have been successful on this course with previous players.

ROBERT on a particular hole shared with me, "If he hit a shot in this area, that I was able to give him some attitude."

At this site, we were allowed to ride a cart for the pace of play. I made sure ROBERT played at a pace he was comfortable with, walking, riding, whatever it took. Some t-boxes were required for both of us to ride.

The hole we had discussed to not hit in a particular area, well, he hit a shot that led to a double bogey! ROBERT was four over, yes four over after eight holes, and the ninth hole to the tenth tee was about a mile it seemed.

As we left the ninth green, ROBERT was pissed, angry, pouting, and just over-the-top negative! So I took a course of action that was a bit unusual. I drove to my car, and ROBERT asked me, "What are you doing?" I replied, "I'm leaving, good luck because you have a defeative attitude and we have sixty-three holes left for you to qualify." The look on his face was indescribable, he had never had anyone do that before but guess what, he finished five under for the tournament and tied for fifth comfortably qualifying!

The following year, ROBERT asked me if I would caddy for the LA OPEN qualifying. I have had tremendous success at RIVIERA at the LA OPEN.

So we played a course that I was not familiar with in the Los Angeles area, but I did my homework and so did ROBERT. He birdied the first hole, which always gets you going, and then birdied the second. ROBERT was on fire but kept within himself. He was flag hunting all day, one of the best balls striking days I have ever seen!

ROBERT had at least twelve putts within ten feet for birdie, and seven putts within five feet and could not make one! Twelve putts, he makes half of those putts, he shoots a sixty-four! So I finally said to his future wife walking off the fifteenth hole after she made some comment to me that "ROBERT has to have some form of divine intervention in his game! It's unfortunate that the truth hurts!"

GARY HALLBERG, TONY SILLS, ROBIN FREEMAN

I had the opportunity to start working on the PGA TOUR when a doctor friend of mine spoke to me about working with a PGA TOUR friend who had some difficulty on the TOUR. The player was GARY HALLBERG.

GARY was the first NCAA golfer to be named four-time first team ALL-AMERICAN from WAKE FOREST. His teammates were SCOTT HOCH, CURTIS STRANGE, and a few others.

Our first PGA TOUR event was the PHOENIX OPEN.

I monitored HALLBERG'S heart rate in our practice rounds and determined his comfortable playing heart rate.

GARY played solidly the first few days and put us into position being the final group to tee off on Sunday. I walked to the tee for our starting tee time without my player in tow.

The starter told me HALLBERG only has two minutes to tee. The other players were inquiring, "Where is he?"

I said, "He was just finishing his warm-up on the stationary bike in the PGA TOUR FITNESS TRAILER." "WHAT!" was the response from our playing partners and caddies in our group. MARK CALCAVECHIA started laughing, I thought that was ironic from a "FAT GUY" who looked like he hasn't turned down a good meal or a beer he didn't like!

CAROL MANN had tuned in to what I was saying and inquired about what was going on. I told her, "I get my player in his playing heart rate, so it doesn't take four holes to get into playing rhythm."

CAROL was the PGA TOUR on-course commentator for radio.

CAROL approached me and asked me, "What was going on?"

I shared with her that HALLBERG is ten under par on the first four holes for the first three days, and we were in the final group!

NO ONE HAD EVER HEARD OF A TRAINOR, NUTRITIONIST, BUSINESS OWNER, CADDY. I WAS THE FIRST!

We were tied after the turn. I have to admit that as a rookie caddie, I "started thinking about my cut of the winner's check!"

The crowd was at least one hundred thousand and on SUPER BOWL Sunday. The tournament today has a record-breaking crowd, and the sixteenth par 3 is a spectator must, sixty thousand, and a raucous crowd!

CALCAVECHIA was on fire being seven under on the back nine, and we had a top ten finish! I learned my lesson to NOT think about the result but focus on the task at hand.

On the final hole, HALLBERG hit his second shot into the trap in front of the green. GARY hit a poor shot and abruptly tossed me his club unexpectedly where I dove to prevent a penalty stroke (not applying today) to the laughter of about twenty thousand spectators!

So at the end of the round, I had to get to LOS ANGELES, and RIVIERA COUNTRY CLUB for our next tournament.

I didn't have a radio in my car and the fast-food worker who I spoke with when ordering food thought I was from MARS when I inquired, "Who won the SUPER BOWL?"

Got to the course that BEN HOGAN and some of the biggest names had historic runs at this track early.

Unfortunately, it was a wet tournament week. We had to play twenty-nine holes on Saturday to get the tournament back on schedule. I had tweaked my ankle the week before in my diving sand trap performance, and my ankle was swollen beyond recognition of my own anatomy part.

I love this course and its location!

We finished in the top twenty and are now prepared for our next tournament to start in PEBBLE BEACH.

During this time, I still owned a small restaurant business that I had to monitor.

Got to PEBBLE, this is a course I had played numerous times and felt I knew this course better than I know most people.

GARY was a different guy! He walked at an angle to prevent drag on his body from the wind, and also told me, "To walk further away from him so he wouldn't be pulled into my draft." Seriously, BIZARRE!

We made the cut and had to tee on ten to start our Sunday round. meaning that we were an afterthought! We made the turn closing with two birdies on the front nine, seventeenth and eighteenth holes. During our first three holes, GARY birdied two more holes, and we appeared on the bottom of the tournament board.

On the fourth hole, one of the most photographed golf holes in the world, his future wife wanted to take photos of GARY. I noticed GARY stopping and posing for a photo. This was during the final round of a PGA TOUR event where he had birdied four of the last five holes!

So then I noticed her telling him, "To move to an area for a better backdrop photo." I'm thinking, "Does she know he is moving up the leaderboard?"

I took the unusual action to slow down and walk right next to him, stop if he stopped for a photo opportunity, and get his head back to the task at hand.

So he finished with seven birdies in the last ten holes at PEBBLE BEACH and finished in the top twenty! From nowhere to making the leaderboard! On our ride in the tournament car, MIKE HULBERT, our playing partner, said about HALLBERGS' future wife said, "He had NEVER seen that in a PGA tournament where a player stopped for photo opportunities when he was a birdie machine!"

At the end of the round, the three of us gathered off the course. His future wife asked, "Why I would step into pictures that she wanted to take of GARY?" I said without any hesitation, "This is GARY'S job, and he needs to acquire the most money possible to retain his card for next year's playing privileges, and he had seven birdies in the final ten holes!"

Obviously, I ended my caddying with GARY and return to 10S players.

Years later, GARY was in the desert and wanted to attend my ex-wife's rehearsal dinner at BIGHORN COUNTRY CLUB. According to ROBIN FREEMAN'S wife, he called three to four times to her to be invited.

She told him yes but he had to bring an expensive gift!

ROBIN FREEMAN

We drove my SUV on a summer PGA TOUR schedule.

From TENNESSEE (first tourney and first win), OHIO, KANSAS, SOUTH DAKOTA, IOWA, NEBRASKA, PENNSYLVANIA, NEW YORK, WASHINGTON D.C., LOUISIANA, TEXAS, throughout CALIFORNIA, and occasionally would park at the airport and grab a flight!

I remember we were trying to get to DC from the south. We both agreed after looking at a map to take the back-country roads of WEST VIRGINIA and VIRGINIA to get to D.C. I have to say I felt like I was on the back roads from the movie *Deliverance*! I saw some things that I only thought we would see in a movie.

ROBIN'S wife's parents were professional athletes. Her father was PITTSBURGH PIRATES HALL OF FAMER, RALPH KINER, and her mother was tennis player NANCY CHAFFEE. So ROBIN'S wife had high expectations! She wanted ROBIN to have a career like ARNOLD PALMER, GREG NORMAN, or even JACK. KC was tough but drove him also over the edge sometimes with her comments on how to be a successful golfer.

ROBIN was a good guy and a GREAT father to two sons who both graduated from CLEMSON UNIVERSITY. I am just sorry that they really didn't know how tough it is to keep their card on the PGA TOUR.

ROBIN tried to qualify for the CHAMPIONS PGA TOUR. I remember he was playing the final round and was within his goal with four holes left. THE CHAMPIONS TOUR qualifying is the most challenging and difficult qualifying school. The CHAMPIONS TOUR only takes five players for playing privileges, the toughest tour to qualify.

He was two strokes safely to qualify for the CHAMPIONS TOUR, except ROBIN finished four over for the last four holes and missed by one stroke.

CHAMPIONS TOUR is a GREAT TOUR with all your bubs!

TONY SILLS

Interesting guy!

He won his only tourney at THE HOUSTON OPEN in a playoff against GREG NORMAN and SEVE BALLESTEROS. The CRYSTAL CHAMPIONSHIP TROPHY was displayed at my business for years.

He asked me to caddy for him at a NATIONWIDE TOUR event. TONY had NOT made a cut all year playing in twelve events.

He was a good guy with a strange sense of dry humor that I understood.

In our practice round on a course that was up and down similar to where the INTERNATIONAL in DENVER, COLORADO.

Going up and down in difficult terrain, TONY demanded that "The clubs shouldn't clang or make any noise!" Trust me, I took every step to keep the clubs from making any noise by wrapping clubs with an additional towel, etc.

He kept verbally assaulting my carrying of the clubs as the other guys were laughing about how ridiculous it was. I finally just dropped the bag going up and down through the brush and said, "I am out of here!"

It was a practice round, but I wasn't going to put up with his crap on a demanding mountain course. It was absurd! I gave him my honest wrath and said, "Maybe this is one of the reasons why you have not made a cut all year and why you have had different caddies for every event. You should be concentrating on the task at hand, your next shot!"

We came to an understanding and he focused on the task at hand. He made his one and only cut and finished in the top twenty.

TONY became a sales spokesperson for the "SEE-MORE" putter and signed his good buddy PAYNE STEWART. The future looked bright after PAYNE won the U.S. OPEN at PINEHURST (I caddied at U.S. OPEN the year he won) and unfortunately, we all knew about the tragic loss of the unbelievable PAYNE STEWART. "SEE-MORE" putter went away.

VIJAY SINGH

I have never seen a player work so hard on his game than VIJAY SINGH. I was happy I never caddied for him because he seemed to be on the course or practice area 24/7. The caddy embraced his short off-season!

DAVID DUVAL

I was in NEW ORLEANS having breakfast in the player's dining area and just relaxing before our round.

I was asked if the seats at my table were taken by DAVID DUVAL. I said no, and DUVAL pulled out a chair and sat down.

I shared with him, "My mother verified his fifty-nine at PGA WEST, BOB HOPE DESERT CLASSIC because she was the head of scoring on SUNDAY CHAMPIONSHIP round."

We laughed, and I told him who I was caddying for and continued to have GREAT conversation about snowboarding, and everything but not golf! He was such a good guy.

BEN CRENSHAW

What a GREAT guy! I was looping on the eleventh hole at RIVIERA COUNTRY CLUB, and BEN was the on-course reporter. He approached me from behind and asked me how we were doing. My guy was in contention and just hit the on-course bathroom.

BEN was pleasant and shared with me, "When you got to go, you got to go out here." I told him, "Yesterday I had to relieve myself and found it amusing when you approach the toilet with lots of spectators carrying a bag. They depart the seas to give you a quick relief." The looks are always funny!

MOTEL 6 - PINEHURST, NC #1234

23331610

MCWILLIAMS	RANDY				
Last	First				
US OPEN CADDIE		129	25878	2/0	
Company/Group		Room #	Folio #	Adult/Child	
		06/13/99	06/20/99	RACK	
		Arrive	Depart	Rate Type	
		65.99	5.94	503.51	
		Rate/Night	Tax/Night	Total Est. Charge	

Description	Charges	Credits
VISA/MC	503.51	503.51
		—

Date	Room
06/13/99	129

FOR RESERVATIONS NATIONWIDE, CALL 1-800-4-MOTEL 6

NOTICE TO GUEST:
This property is privately owned. Management reserves the right to refuse service to anyone and will not be responsible for the loss of money, jewelry or valuables of any kind.
RATES ARE SUBJECT TO APPLICABLE TAXES AND MAY CHANGE WITHOUT ADVANCE NOTICE

JACK NICKLAUS, ARNOLD PALMER, GARY PLAYER

The "BIG 3" of "GOLF!"

These icons made golf what it is today! Even before the "TIGER" effect!

I have met all three on numerous occasions and spent time with two of the three and admit that the three times I crossed paths with "ARNIE," it was non-eventful!

ARNIE spent a lot of time in the COACHELLA VALLEY, he was a regular at various restaurants/country clubs and was like a "FAVORITE SON CELEBRITY ATHLETE."

From SHERWOOD COUNTRY CLUB to COACHELLA VALLEY. He was a close friend and confident buddy of FREDDIE COUPLES.

GARY PLAYER did more for the country of SOUTH AFRICA than almost any famous SOUTH AFRICAN politician! He was a pioneer of race, politics, employment, real estate, and GOLF! He loves horses as well!

GARY was a humanitarian even to this day!

Our first interaction was at a tournament at PGA WEST where I lived. GARY PLAYER had just signed a contract for a golf course design development in COLORADO where I was employed as a consultant.

GARY PLAYER had just had hernia surgery and I gave him a rehab program for his recovery.

GRAY PLAYER is one of my all-time favorites!

Read about the "KING" the "GOAT," the GREATEST OF ALL TIME in "SHARK SHOOTOUT" and "SHERWOOD COUNTRY CLUB!"

LEE TREVINO

One is practicing on the driving range at THE CITRUS course in LA QUINTA, CALIFORNIA GARY HALLBERG was joined by TOM WATSON, LEE TREVINO, HOLLIS STACY.

We were on the western driving range for pros only.

I had a video camera and took footage of stroke production. The T was elevated, about ten feet and ventured in direct line with players hitting shots—remember the T was elevated!

I stood in front and got the camera rolling, and TREVINO was taking aim. WATSON said, "You're brave standing in front of TREVINO." And I said, "You're pros, you better not hit me."

PETER JACOBSON

"MR. PERSONALITY," "MR. OREGON," a bonus marketing of the PGA TOUR!

We met at "THE SHARK SHOOTOUT," and our personalities meshed very well! I picked him up off his feet, he was shocked that I could pick him up so easily!

We had so much fun, we loved music and embraced life!

The following week, PETER and his family came to the desert for "THE SKIN'S GAME" and he surprisingly came into my restaurant when it was closed and wanted breakfast even though I was not open to the public. I charged him for breakfast. I have always learned that I am in business and have to pay for a product to stay open.

Throughout the years, I would have so many household sports named athletes who would venture in, they make "BIG BUCKS" and can buy a $10 breakfast!

The following year, I ran into PETER at "QUAD CITIES OPEN." He gave me a shout-out, hug, and conversed until we had our t-time. My player was asking as we walked down the #1 fairway how we knew each other. PETER was a talented person, including singing in a band with PAYNE STEWART.

LANNY WADKINS

LANNY WADKINS was part of our threesome at THE HOUSTON OPEN on SUNDAY. We were chatting after our second shot on a par 5 when LANNY said, "I am going to get an ice cream. Does anyone want one?" My player said, "Buy my guy an ice cream bar." And he walked back to the group with his ice cream bar happily and gave me an ice cream that I ate in two minutes!

That was a first and only!

U.S. OPEN

From the EAST coast to the WEST coast!

CONGRESSIONAL, PEBBLE BEACH, and PINEHURST. The year that PAYNE STEWART won his last major and passed in a tragic accident.

My parents took me to watch KEN VENTURI at CONGRESSIONAL and the U.S. OPEN.

As a little guy with so much energy and restlessness, I was hard to manage.

I still remember being in trouble because KEN VENTURI turned toward my folks and asked them to quiet the little guy "Mois." I shared with him this story since he lived in our area.

Years later, I attended the U.S. OPEN at PEBBLE BEACH where TOM WATSON drained a shot on seventeenth hole to give him a lead over JACK NICKLAUS and win the U.S. OPEN

Then once again at PEBBLE BEACH and the U.S. OPEN, TIGER WOODS won the U.S. OPEN by a runaway. I have NEVER seen a course set up so differently than the course usually played. The greens were the smallest ever! USGA set up!

For one year, my cousin's husband led the open at THE BLACK course in NEW YORK, RICKY BARNES. His brother caddied for him and the pressure led to his demise with about five holes left. My parents along with some of the club members, where RICKY'S family belongs, help sponsor him.

Then I caddied at the U.S. OPEN at PINEHURST where PAYNE STEWART won the OPEN and the embrace by PAYNE TO PHIL MICKELSON congratulating him on becoming a father where that was more important than any golf tournament.

TIGER WOODS

I first followed TIGER when he was in high school. I would follow TIGER because the high school player I was working with seemed to always be in his tournament group. Actually, my guy had a winning record in match play against TIGER. My guy went onto PEPPERDINE and contributed to PEPPERDINE winning the NCAA CHAMPIONSHIPS.

Then RIVIERA, as a sixteen-year-old amateur, TIGER was granted an opportunity to play in the field.

I pointed out to my player how packed the t-box area was in anticipation of TIGER'S debut.

Then I also was caddying at TIGER'S pro-debut at the QUAD CITIES OPEN in DAVENPORT/MOLINE, ILLINOIS.

Then at U.S. OPEN at PEBBLE BEACH, he demonstrated his future dominance by running away with the title on the course GOD built. I grew up in the SOUTH BAY/MONTEREY and spent numerous days at PEBBLE BEACH GOLF LINKS, and "YOU WILL NEVER see anyone that will play four rounds against the world's top golfers again with a *W* like that again!"

I went to the WESTERN OPEN in CHICAGO, with a few of the top junior golfers. They wanted to see TIGER and the possibility of getting an autograph like the other thousands of fans.

So I was positioned on the path TIGER had to take off the eighteenth green with ten deep from the green to the scorers' area. How could I get TIGER'S attention? So from about twenty feet away, I joined the chorus of spectators shouting his name for an autograph or anything.

"How about an autograph for a STANFORD INDIAN?" (What STANFORD was called before having to be politically correct and changed from INDIANS to CARDINAL)

I could see that he heard the unusual call out.

Then I said, "How about an autograph for a former player I worked with as coach?" (TIGER very seldom beat this player growing up in the juniors in match play), then he slowed down and looked in my direction, he said, "What are you doing on that side of the ropes?" And he asked their names and signed two programs for my guys. They were in heaven!

It was interesting for people trying to figure out why TIGER signed our programs. At this time, his contract only allowed him to sign so many autographs daily if he signed any at all!

TIGER never met a TELEVISION camera he didn't like!

Years later, he had a FALLING from grace, then rose again like a soaring "Phoenix."

TIGER playing made a lot of PGA players very wealthy!

CHAPTER 3

MUSICIANS

"MUSIC IS PLAYING INSIDE MY HEAD"
"SINATRA" TOO "ROCK and ROLL"

We ask ourselves a question, "What would our world be like without music?" Music moves our soul, mind, spirit, heart, emotions, and most importantly, our lives. The world would be a far different place if we did not have music in our lives.

WHAT IS THE DEFINITION OF MUSIC?

The science or art of ordering tones or sounds of succession, in combination, and in temporal relationships to produce a composition having unity and continuity. Vocal, instrumental, or mechanical sounds having rhythm, melody, or harmony, choral music, etc.

I have been singing, dancing, entertaining, playing, and surrounded by sound all my life! As a child, I was in a church choir, and my parents sang and played the piano, sang and played love songs to each other, and introduced me to the piano. I played drums or tapped to anything I could drum too.

My father during college was occasionally hired as security (all the bigger football players were offered this), and then one night, the manager asked if anyone knew of a drummer who could step in for the night. "LIONEL HAMPTON" was the marque. Anyway, my father said, "YES, I PLAY THE SKINS." And sure enough, he stepped in and performed admirably. This ALL-AMERICAN COLLEGE ATHLETE was the talk of the campus for the next few weeks.

"LITTLE STEVIE WONDER"

My first real exposure to music came at CARRS BEACH on the CHESAPEAK BAY in MARYLAND. This was 1964. CARRS BEACH was a venue for people of color, black specifically and no whites. The beach venue was protected by barbed-wire fence out into the CHESAPEAK BAY about a quarter mile. My two young friends (we were ten to twelve years of age) and I were playing on the beach and ventured to an area that most people did not go to (especially whites). The tide was low, and we swam and walked to the barrier of barbed wire in the bay. We had heard of the young musical genius playing and performing talented and had the crowd's attention (No one saw us inside the barbed-wire fence, we were too small). This was my first concert with "LITTLE STEVIE WONDER." I still remember my experiences to this day. I often wondered why NO ONE ever produced a documentary about this venue? One of the GREATEST albums ever produced, *Songs in the Key of Life*. And my favorite tune of the many GREAT songs he produced is "Heaven Is 10 Zillion Light Years Away." I sang, "My Cherie Amour" with a full forty-piece orchestra opening for a benefit concert in INDIAN WELLS, DESERT HORIZONS where the headliners were DINAH CARROLL and VIC DAMONE. "GOD" graced us with "LITTLE STEVIE WONDER!"

LOUIS "SATCHMO" ARMSTRONG

At STANFORD UNIVERSITY, I volunteered to help with an event that included the iconic LOUIS ARMSTRONG (explained in the celebrity chapter) who was more than you can imagine. He was inviting and charismatic, and little did he know I would make my first dance at my wedding to his recorded tune from *Sleepless in Seattle*. My marriage lasted for seven years. I had "SLEEPLESS NIGHTS IN PALM DESERT." One of the GREATEST performers in his era and to this day.

"THE CHAIRMAN OF THE BOARD"

FRANK SINATRA (articles and story in celebrity section) lived in RANCHO MIRAGE ON FRANK SINATRA STREET. He and his wife were very active in our community. I attended many various events that were in honor of the SINATRAS throughout our valley. The most memorable was being shown all of "THE CHAIRMAN of the BOARD'S" private wine/liquor room, his private train collection, and most importantly his GOLD RECORD framed music collection.

HAL BLAINE

"WRECKING CREW"

The Wrecking Crew is the iconic studio musician who contributed to many of today's most memorable recordings. *Ghost* plays to such hits, "Mr. Tambourine Man" by The Byrds. The first two albums of The Monkees, and "Pet Sounds" by the Beach Boys that many consider the GREATEST album ever recorded. They also played on hits for "FRANK SINATRA," "NANCY SINATRA," "SONNY and CHER," "JAN and DEAN," "GARY LEWIS & the PLAYBOYS," "THE MAMAS & THE PAPAS," "TIJUANA BRASS," "RICKY NELSON," "JOHNNY RIVERS," and too many hits to name with "PHIL SPECTOR'S WALL OF SOUND."

HAL BLAINE is a member of "THE ROCK & ROLL HALL of FAME," "TEC HALL OF FAME," "THE PERCUSSION HALL of FAME," "MODERN DREAMER'S HALL of FAME," "NASHVILLE HALL of FAME," and "CLASSIC DRUMMER'S HALL of FAME."

Such hits with the following artists to name a few, from "MACARTHUR PARK," **_RICHARD HARRIS_**, "ROMEO and JULIET," **_HENRY MANCINI_**, "SAN FRANCISCO," **_SCOTT MACKENZIE_**, "THAT'S LIFE," **_FRANK SINATRA_**, (too many to list) "WAY WE WERE," **_BARBRA STREISAND_**, "ALONG COMES MARY," "CHERISH," **_THE ASSOCIATION_**, "ANNIE'S SONG," "CALYPSO," "ROCKY MOUNTAIN HIGH," **_JOHN DENVER_**, "AQUARIUS," "UP-UP AND AWAY," **_THE FIFTH DIMENSION_**, "MRS. ROBINSON," "CECILIA," "BRIDGE OVER TROUBLED WATERS," "ALL I KNOW," "AMERICA," "THE BOXER," "SOUNDS OF SILENCE," **_SIMON and GARFUNKEL_**, "CALIFORNIA DREAMIN'," "HELP ME RHONDA," "IN MY ROOM," "BARBARA ANN," "GOOD VIBRATIONS," "LITTLE DEUCE COUPE," "I GET AROUND," "DANCE DANCE DANCE," **_BEACH BOYS_**, "GALVESTON," "BY THE TIME I GET TO PHOENIX," "WICHITTA LINEMEN," **_GLEN CAMPBELL_**, "CALIFORNIA DREAMIN'," "DEDICATED TO THE ONE I

LOVE," "MONDAY, MONDAY," ***THE MAMAS & THE PAPAS***, "VENTURA HIGHWAY," "MUSKRAT MUSKRAT," "HORSE WITH NO NAME," ***AMERICA***, over 35,000 sounds he recorded with artists. Some of my favorite tunes.

HAL lived in PALM DESERT around the corner from my business. He enjoyed entertaining my guests with his stories and quick wit and sharp tongue. He always like sharing jokes with Melissa, and they always had a sexy tone to them. He drove an old Cadillac with the license plates reading DRUMMER. Unfortunately, he lost most of his fortune, he passed away at ninety, but his music will have a long-lasting place in your heart!

GLEN CAMPBELL

"WRECKING CREW"

He had a passion to play golf whenever the opportunity arise in pro-ams such as the former BOB HOPE CLASSIC.

I was caddying for a professional (story in golf chapter) at INDIAN WELLS COUNTRY CLUB, and we were practicing on the range for our round.

All of a sudden, GLEN CAMPBELL asked if there was a spot open next to us on the range. I said sure. After a few minutes, I asked him how he liked the desert? He answered, "How could you not?" My player got involved chatting with some locals, so I sat down on the driving range right behind where GLEN CAMPBELL was hitting balls. I asked him, "What is JIMMY WEBB up to?" He looked at me with curiosity. "He is special," he said. I told him I had a few of his albums and shared that he was a talented songwriter. GLEN CAMPBELL's GREATEST hits were written by JIMMY WEBB so GLEN sat down with me and we chatted. He asked me about caddying, music, etc. I told him about my businesses. The following morning, he saw me as we were heading to the tee for our starting time, and our local paper wrote an article about me and he said, "Nice article." GLEN CAMPBELL was also a member of the "WRECKING CREW" until he became a star. He left his mark in our hearts and minds with his recordings.

KINGSTON TRIO

My oldest brother played the acoustic guitar, and one of his favorite groups was "THE KINGSTON TRIO." BOB SHANE went to MENLO COLLEGE in MENLO PARK, CALIFORNIA.

He sang and played most of their songs such as "Where Have All the Flowers Gone," "Lemon Tree," "500 Miles," "Hang Down Your Head Tom Dooley." So it was a big thrill for me to have the last surviving member of "THE KINGSTON TRIO" come in for breakfast at my business. "BOB SHANE," they had 5 #1 albums!

"THE KINGSTON TRIO" made an annual trip at Christmastime to play at our wonderful McCALLUM THEATER venue. I shared that I performed at the same venue when it first opened, and I sang "500 Miles" for my audition.

You might wonder how I got to perform at the theater? I was shopping at a grocery store listening to music with my headphones on and singing to EMERSON, LAKE, & PALMER'S "Just Take a Pebble." As I approached checking out, a man approached me and asked if I sing professionally. I answered, "Only in the shower." He laughed and introduced himself as the music director for the opening of the new theater and then asked, "Would you like to audition for the first cast production at the theater?"

The music director happened to see an article in our local newspaper about me and visited my business that day. He announced who he was and asked if I would like to audition right on the spot. I had customers who encouraged me to sing since I sang along to the music that I always had on.

I showed up and sang an assortment of tunes, octapello, which included "500 Miles" and got a major role performing four musical numbers.

I shared this with BOB, and he got a real kick out of my story. I even gave him a quick sample of my voice! "500 MILES" and "WHERE HAVE ALL THE FLOWERS GONE." He and his girlfriend and future wife got a kick, and laughed about it.

Before he left, I asked him if he would leave a voicemail on my brother's phone since "THE KINGSTON TRIO" had an impact on his music. Sure enough, he called and left a message.

The following year, "KINGSTON TRIO" made their annual pilgrimage to the Palm Desert.

BOB, being the only surviving member of the original "KINGSTON TRIO," would always perform two songs with the new version of the group. He would sing a random tune but always sing, "SCOTCH and SODA." At this time, unfortunately, BOB had an oxygen tank to assist him with a respiratory issue.

He brought me a gift box set of "KINGSTON TRIO" autographed and signed. Additionally, PBS television network was on hand documenting BOB and being a member of the "HALL OF FAME KINGSTON TRIO."

He passed away the following year. I think of him every day, his autographed box set CD is on my wall as I enter and exit my kitchen! What a TERRIFIC man!

CROSBY, STILLS, NASH, and YOUNG

Where do I start? The first "SUPER GROUP!"

DAVID CROSBY is a member of the "THE BYRDS" with members including ROGER McGUINN.

STEPHEN STILLS is a member of the "BUFFALO SPRINGFIELD" with members NEIL YOUNG, RICHIE FURAY, BRUCE PALMER, JIM MESSINA, DEWEY MARTIN. People recognize this as one of the first original "SUPER GROUPS."

GRAHAM NASH is a member of "THE HOLLIES" and "CROSBY and NASH."

NEIL YOUNG is a member of "BUFFALO SPRINGFIELD" and a group I heard for its brief existence "THE DUCKS" in SANTA CRUZ.

"THE HOLLIES" had great harmonies with GRAHAM NASH who was the silent leader and most recognized member of the band. GRAHAM NASH was a visionary to help form this superstar group.

GRAHAM NASH lives in ENCINO HILLS in SOUTHERN CALIFORNIA.

STEPHEN STILLS was the guitarist leader of the band. A member of the supergroup "BUFFALO SPRINGFIELD," who brought the harmony of the guitar sound.

DAVID CROSBY of "THE BYRDS" was the edge who made things smooth, and his lyrics of delivery were fabulous. Unfortunately, we will address the future.

NEIL YOUNG also of "BUFFALO SPRINGFIELD" was the secret addition to make this ensemble the "SUPER GROUP" at the time.

My first live experience with Neil Young was in 1973 when he played at SANTA CRUZ AUDITORIUM. The venue was very small, sat six hundred, was the first for NEIL YOUNG to introduce him to SANTA CRUZ.

The opening act was the rising future star LINDA RONSTADT and the STONE PONIES. At one time, her backup band was later known as the EAGLES. Members were GLENN FREY, DON HENLEY. LINDA RONSTADT was the opening act for NEIL YOUNG.

NEIL YOUNG had just released the commercially successful "HARVEST" the year before. NEIL YOUNG curtailed his live shows due to a nagging back injury. The band members included drummer JOHNNY BARBATA, a multi-talented piano placer, etc., JACK NITZSCHE, and steel player BEN KEITH—they all formed NEIL YOUNG'S band.

They rocked with an electric performance bringing the house alive, and my favorite tune "THE LONER," then classics "OLD MAN," "HEART of GOLD," then GRAHAM NASH and DAVID CROSBY brought their electric guitars and rocked the small group with "ALABAMA," "SOUTHERN MAN," "CINNAMON GIRL." To this day, they are probably the top three of my all-time concerts.

CSNY disbanded but got together for a reunion concert with the opening show in SEATTLE, WASHINGTON. I had GREAT seats, and it was a very commercially successful show.

Then in 1977, NEIL YOUNG lived in the area and formed a group called NEIL YOUNG and THE DUCKS with local rockers. They played regularly at "THE CATALYST."

I managed a restaurant on the water in SANTA CRUZ YACHT HARBOR. It was a Saturday night, and we closed the dining room at 9:00 p.m. I got called out to the dining room from my closing paperwork and was asked if we could serve a small table dinner.

The table consisted of NEIL YOUNG, CARRIE SNODGRASS (NEIL'S honey), JOHNNY BARBATA, JACK NITZSCHE, and CALVIN SAMUELS, and someone else. They wanted dinner one-and-a-half hours after we stopped seating people. I went back to our cook, BOB DUBOIS, and closing waiter, JIMMY GUIERRO, to see if they would like to re-open and wait on their table. Of course, I said you might get an autographed album and a big tip!

So we presented the check to NEIL YOUNG which came to $250 and some change. (A lot in those days). I picked up the check with about a $5 tip. I reapproached the table and said, "We re-opened our kitchen and grill, kept a waiter on to serve you, you had wine and drinks, everything was OK from our end, and we all have your albums." NEIL YOUNG grabbed me by my necktie and pulled me into his face neighborhood and said, "MO, CURLEY, and LARRY don't give a damn." I pulled myself away from him and said, "WHAT THE HELL?" And he repeated the THREE STOOGES comment. I will NEVER forget this!

NEIL YOUNG married DARYL HANNAH, the actress in *Splash* and *Kill Bill* franchise, after a four-year dating relationship. DAVID CROSBY originally said some controversial things about their relationship, and they have not spoken since.

DAVID CROSBY, my FAVORITE of CSN & Y!

One evening, I was working at a restaurant called the SHADOWBROOK located on the CAPITOLA RIVER, near SANTA CRUZ. It was a five-star and recognized as one of the most historic restaurants in the world. A small stream flowed through the restaurant, and a cable car would bring you down the hill to the dining area, beautiful gardens, and overlooking the river.

Multi-leveled with a small two-top table on the landing as you walked to the main dining room. Very romantic and cozy, and you have a great view of the dining area below. The restaurant was built in '30s, and you NEVER see anything like this.

My first time rubbing elbows with CROSBY was when he sat at that table with JONI MITCHELL. I had a nice exchange and a very pleasant one.

I bought tickets for my birthday and friends to a concert in DAVID CROSBY'S hometown in MARIN, CALIFORNIA. I paid for the best seats possible, center stage third row.

DAVID CROSBY came on to stage with guitars on a stand and a grand piano front and center. CROSBY sat down to play his fourth song, "GUINNEVERE," an absolutely gorgeous ballad. During a verse, someone yelled out, "NICE SOCKS." He was wearing two different colors of socks. CROSBY stopped playing and looked in the direction of the person's outburst. He got up from the piano and walked off the stage and ended his show. It was a very expensive evening for me.

DAVID CROSBY was railroaded by his former bandmates and a few others due to some very bad choices. You should watch the documentary "DAVID CROSBY," the documentary sets the record straight.

STEPHEN STILLS is still an unbelievable guitarist, his solo and group work is what legends are made of.

CROSBY, STILLS, and NASH played recently at an INDIAN CASINO in INDIO, CALIFORNIA. My friend got me seats in the tribal area, basically the front ten rows. Before I sat down, I asked the sound man, "Could I look at their song list for the evening?"

The show started. After a few tunes, CROSBY said, "We have 1,000+ songs between us and we are going to sing a song from another artist which is unusual for us." And seating so close, I raised my voice and said, "BLACKBIRD," a BEATLES song. CROSBY gave me a puzzled look, "Isn't this guy clairvoyant?"

MONTEREY POP FESTIVAL–1967

ERIC BURDON, COUNTRY JOE McDONALD, DAVID CROSBY, TOM SMOTHERS, JERRY GARCIA, PIGPEN, GRACE SLICK. Little did I know what the future would bring of me having moments of association with these artists from this concert line-up.

My parents had a beach house in Aptos, California. A group of my high school friends went for the weekend to my parent's pad with the intention of attending MONTEREY POP FESTIVAL.

Calmer heads prevailed since my father voted against letting us go to the FESTIVAL since none of us were not old enough to drive. My father did not want to interrupt his golf weekend at APTOS SEASCAPE.

The first successful mega concert! The headliner was the "MAMA and the PAPAS." Check out the line-up.

THE ASSOCIATION, THE PAUPERS, LOU RAWLS, BEVERLY, JOHNNY RIVERS, ERIC BURDON and THE ANIMALS*, SIMON and GARFUNKEL, CANNED HEAT, BIG BROTHER and THE HOLDING COMPANY, THE PAUL BUTTERFIELD BLUES BAND, ELECTRIC FLAG, MOBY GRAPE, HUGH MASEKELA, THE BYRDS, LAURA NYRO, JEFFERSON AIRPLANE, BOOKER T. and the M.G.'S, OTIS REDDING, BLUES PROJECT, BUFFALO SPRINGFIELD, THE WHO, THE GRATEFUL DEAD, THE JIMI HENDRIX EXPERIENCE, THE MAMA'S and the PAPA'S, SCOTT McKENZIE.

TOM SMOOTHERS was the MC introducing some of the acts at this historic event. Our paths would cross later in SANTA CRUZ where they have a winery with DICK SMOOTHERS. He is probably one of the greatest yo-yo players of all time! DICK SMOOTHERS had the hots for my girlfriend!

WOODSTOCK–1969

TIM HARDIN, JOAN BAEZ, RICHIE HAVENS, COUNTRY JOE McDONALD, JOHN B. SEBASTIAN, JERRY GARCIA, GRACE SLICK, DAVID CROSBY, GRAHAM NASH, NEIL YOUNG. Once again, little did I know what the future would bring of me having an association with these artists who performed at the most iconic concerts of my era.

RICHIE HAVENS, SWEETWATER, TIM HARDIN, RVI SHANKAR, MELANIE SAFKA, BERT SOMMER, ARLO GUTHRIE, JOAN BAEZ, SRI SWAMI SATCHIDANANDA, QUILL, COUNTRY JOE McDONALD, SANTANA, JOHN B. SEBASTIAN, KEEF HARTLEY BAND, THE INCREDIBLE STRING BAND, CANNED HEAT, MOUNTAIN, THE GRATEFUL DEAD, CREDENCE CLEARWATER REVIVAL, THE WHO, JEFFERSON AIRPLANE, JOE COCKER, COUNTRY JOE and THE FISH, JANIS JOPLIN, TEN YEARS AFTER, THE BAND, JOHNNY WINTER, SLY and THE FAMILY STONE, BLOOD, SWEAT & TEARS, CROSBY, STILLS, and NASH, PAUL BUTTERFIELD BLUES BAND, SHA NA NA, JIMI HENDRIX.

I lived in SANTA CRUZ, CALIFORNIA, and the town had a venue called the Catalyst which had live music nightly.

One of my favorite artists was Tim Hardin who performed at WOODSTOCK, and THE CATALYST where I saw him perform and has a few songs that have now lived in music history. "IF I WERE A CARPENTER," "REASON TO BELIEVE" (ROD STEWART made this a hit), "SIMPLE SONG OF FREEDOM." Unfortunately, he died of an overdose. JOAN BAEZ, PALO ALTO HIGH SCHOOL ALUMNI, read about her in PALO ALTO HIGH SCHOOL musical artists.

RICHIE HAVENS played in another small venue that I was involved in some capacity in SANTA CRUZ. RICHIE HAVENS was an engaging entertaining musician. We talked about numerous things, but most interestingly was his performance at WOODSTOCK.

I lived in SQUAW VALLEY, CALIFORNIA. Known as a ski winter area. During the summer, it was known for its river rafting, hiking, horseback riding, golf, etc., and its entertaining nightlife. I went to "RIVER RANCH" which was at the entrance of ALPINE MEADOWS and just a few miles down the road from SQUAW VALLEY.

Mutual friends from the bay area owned "THE RIVER RANCH," they are the Calhouns. After a wonderful day of river rafting down the Truckee River is where most rafters would end their rafting endeavors at the bar/restaurant/lodge, "THE RIVER RANCH."

I stayed after my glorious day rafting down the Truckee River for dinner and a few beers. Sitting in the packed bar with a small duo of guitar players on stage playing popular tunes. They introduced a guest guitar player joining them for a few tunes WOODSTOCK participant COUNTRY JOE McDONALD.

He sang his famous WOODSTOCK tune, "GIVE ME A F . . . WHAT DOES THAT SPELL?" Out of respect for the mix aged crowd, he didn't use profanity but the bar crowd sang the chant. After his few songs, he saw I had an extra seat and sitting by myself, he asked if he could join me.

Throughout the evening, we shared stories about family, sports, and politics. We met the next evening at the bar for food and libations again. I had some great stories to share when I returned to the bay area.

On the twentieth anniversary of WOODSTOCK, I happened to be in NEW YORK during a break of my coaching. My host had arranged a magazine shoot with about a dozen of NEW YORK'S top young models at "HAGGAR FARM and WOODSTOCK AVIATION BARN MUSEUM." I was the emcee on the bus giving all the models a historical music lesson of the WOODSTOCK music festival. It was interesting that only one model had ever heard of THE WOODSTOCK MUSIC FESTIVAL!

FROST AMPHITHEATER/STANFORD UNIVERSITY WOODSIDE, PALO ALTO, GUNN HIGH SCHOOLS BAY AREA

THE CHAMBERS BROTHERS, QUICKSILVER MESSENGER SERVICE, SANTANA BLUES BAND, CREDENCE CLEARWATER REVIVAL, ELVIN BISHOP, COLD BLOOD, GRATEFUL DEAD, SLY and THE FAMILY STONE, HAIR, SONS of CHAMPLIN, JOY OF COOKING, SPIRIT, JEFFERSON AIRPLANE, IT'S A BEAUTIFUL DAY, PABLO CRUISE, JOAN BAEZ.

FROST AMPHITHEATER is an outside bowl venue that had step seating from top to bottom. Surrounded by tall trees, the sound was second to none with a capacity of eight thousand excluding the tree climbers.

My high school buddies and I always tried to sneak in over/under the fence/barriers or any way possible to get in. I reflect today that tickets were never over $6 bucks, majority $4 bucks to see some of the most historic performances ever.

During the VIETNAM era, there was lots of resistance to the war in our community and especially at STANFORD UNIVERSITY. The student union put on a performance at FROST AMPHITHEATER at 8:00 a.m. that was a HAIR musical. STANFORD student union started the morning with a march to FROST AMPHITHEATER for attendees—it was a GREAT day!

SLY and THE FAMILY STONE performed. SLY canceled numerous concerts, but performed at FROST. SLY and THE FAMILY STONE was GREAT, and knocked their show out of the park! They played a hard-driving set of all their best!

Later in life, SLY had numerous issues and very seldom played live—the night at the Grammy's said it all!

I remember STEVE TYLER and another member of AEROSMITH were scheduled to perform in OAKLAND. They decided to hop on a plane to the GRAMMY'S in LOS ANGELES to have the opportunity to play on stage with the iconic SLY. Lots of fanfare! They were playing their instruments with THE FAMILY STONE'S band members on stage waiting for SLY to appear for the opening tune. SLY walked onto the stage and directly off the stage through the crowd without more than two-to-four words. The look on STEVE TYLER'S face was worth the watching of the show. TYLER got back on their plane and played their concert in OAKLAND. A historical night in the archives of the GRAMMY'S.

PAPA JOHN CREACH, AND HOT TUNA

In the mountains of Santa Cruz, there was this historic lodge in Boulder Creek. The BOULDER CREEK LODGE has a stage where some of the bay area's artists would perform.

I ventured on a rare Saturday night off to listen to "HOT TUNA," a band made up of members of the JEFFERSON AIRPLANE.

PAPA JOHN CREACH was born in 1917 and in his career played with LOUIS ARMSTRONG, NAT KING COLE, FATS WALLER, CHARLIE DANIELS. As I mentioned, PAPA JOHN CREACH was born in 1917, one year earlier than my father.

That evening, I arrived early to get front and center stage. The stage was floor level and all you had to do was extend your arm and take a step, and you were on stage.

PAPA JOHN CREACH and I could shake hands without any hesitation. I danced freely right in front of this amazing violinist musician sweating profusely at a young fifty-nine-year-old musician and he always had a towel on his shoulder while playing his violin.

While he was playing, he had a musical break during a tune, and he extended to me his shoulder towel for me to wipe off all the sweat that I was spraying on to him while dancing directly in front of him.

At the end of the song, I returned the towel to him, thanking him. PAPA JOHN CREECH smiled and said, "You're welcome and glad you are enjoying our music!"

GRACE SLICK AND JEFFERSON AIRPLANE, JEFFERSON STARSHIP

GRACE BARNETT WING or better known as GRACE SLICK of the JEFFERSON AIRPLANE.

Her family moved to my hometown of PALO ALTO in the 1950s, the same time my family returned to PALO ALTO.

GRACIE (a nickname) and WING (SLICK) attended PALO ALTO HIGH SCHOOL where my father was a teacher and then attended and graduated from CASTILLEJA HIGH SCHOOL, an all-girls Catholic school where my mother was the tennis coach/teacher.

I think that finally graduating from this private school and strict discipline contributed to her future entertaining moments in her career.

The tuition in 2021 for CASTILLEJA HIGH SCHOOL is fifty-one thousand dollars!

PALO ALTO HIGH SCHOOL/ATHERTON

JOAN BAEZ, PIGPEN of GRATEFUL DEAD, GRACE SLICK of JEFFERSON AIRPLANE and JEFFERSON STARSHIP, PABLO CRUISE, LINDSEY BUCKINGHAM and STEVIE NICKS of FLEETWOOD MAC.

JOAN BAEZ attended PALO ALTO HIGH SCHOOL in the '50s. My father was a teacher/head Football coach at PALO ALTO HIGH SCHOOL.

JOAN BEAZ performed at WOODSTOCK and MONTEREY POP FESTIVAL. JOAN BAEZ was the first "VIETNAM and GOVERNMENT" activist performer recognized in that era.

JOAN BAEZ married DAVID HARRIS, a proponent of THE VIETNAM WAR. I organized a FORUM at PALY with a panel of eight divided equally is four against/four favoring the WAR in VIETNAM. MILITARY and VIETNAM—very heated forum!

It was brilliant, informative, and entertaining to say the least. DAVID HARRIS provided some fireworks in a colorful exchange of ideas and thoughts and challenges with the pro-VIETNAM.

I remember approaching and introducing myself to JOAN BAEZ. I told her my father was a teacher when she attended PALY. She remembered, and I told her she had the most beautiful skin complexion I had ever seen! Ms. BONNIE HAYDON, DENMARK'S top model and fashion queen, seventy-five, whose daughter married DONALD TRUMP, JR. has the most beautiful skin after thirty years of knowing her story and photos in the celebrity and political chapter. Her secret? Lots of water and doesn't get her DANISH skin in the sun!

ROD "PIGPEN" McKURNEN attended PALO ALTO HIGH SCHOOL and was into music. He died way too soon. He was an original member of "THE GRATEFUL DEAD," his brother was a grade below me and also attended PALO ALTO HIGH SCHOOL.

GRACE SLICK attended PALY as well, but she finished high school at another PALO ALTO school—CASTILLEJA, a private girl's school.

She later was one of the original members of the JEFFERSON AIRPLANE to transform JEFFERSON STARSHIP. She didn't like the later group and quit. The lead singer is MICKEY THOMAS (he also was the front man lead singer of ELVIN BISHOP'S band). GRACE SLICK still lives in the PALO ALTO area and has become a fabulous artist.

I remember we had noon-hour sock hops JOY OF COOKING at lunch hours. They played graduation night. GRATEFUL DEAD played a few times because members attended PALO ALTO HIGH SCHOOL.

IT'S A BEAUTIFUL DAY. LINDA and DAVID LaFLAMME were the first electric violinists. WHITE BIRD, BOMBAY RISING, a great night at WOODSIDE HIGH.

One of the biggest influencers of lead female singers including MADONNA was LYDIA PENCE who attended WOODSIDE HIGH SCHOOL. Her band COLD BLOOD had earth-moving rhythm horn section and a hard-driving sexy soulful sound! LYDIA had every guy wanting to be with her. She is the only artist that let your mind wander and imagine the numerous ways you would spend any time with her.

PABLO CRUISE and CORY LERIOS were the founding members, producers, creative geniuses, and businessmen of one of my favorite groups.

CORY LARIOS was a step ahead of most musicians. He opened a club in SOUTH SHORE LAKE TAHOE on the NEVADA side, CRYSTAL SHIP, and he would book bands at his club. One of the most popular bands he discovered and signed was the CHAMBER BROTHERS. Four brothers and a white drummer. They had numerous hits. TIME HAS COME TODAY.

CORY produced an album WORLD'S AWAY that became the #1 album in the country. They were so big that they had a WALT DISNEY SPECIAL on national television before they were known. My favorite song is OCEAN BREEZE, a masterpiece on their first album!

CORY became the producer of tunes for the nationally syndicated series with over three hundred credits with BAY WATCH. The standard joke was "You never remembered the music, just PAMELA ANDERSON running across the beach."

GREAT GUY! GREAT FATHER! And his two sons are fabulous musicians.

PABLO CRUISE played locally, and I attended and I invited CORY and the band in for breakfast. I expected eight to ten about twenty showed up! I then made him pay. I have always felt bad about that, it's business!

JOHN MCVIE and MICK FLEETWOOD, these two had a house in MAUI and shared a house occasionally with WARREN ZEVON IN THE '70s. Read above.

STEVIE NICKS attended MENLO ATHERTON HIGH SCHOOL, and LINDSEY BUCKINGHAM is where he attended as well. STEVIE was one year apart, he was a senior, LINDSEY a junior.

My girlfriend also went to MENLO ATHERTON at the same time. We connected. My girlfriend and I met at the same place where STEVIE and LINDSEY did "YOUNG LIFE" meetings. I only went to hook up with my future girlfriend, and that was both their intention.

I remember going to LINDSEY BUCKINGHAM'S house on FRIDAYS once in a while for fabulous parties!

MOVIES and MUSIC

HAROLD AND MAUDE, THE BODYGUARD, MONTEREY POP FESTIVAL, THE GRADUATE, WOODSTOCK, BOHEMIAN RHAPSODY.

"WOODSTOCK" the movie speaks for itself and check out my experiences with "WOODSTOCK."

"MONTEREY POP FESTIVAL" same as above except the movie showed that there was an audience for this type of cinema.

"BOHEMIAN RHAPSODY," the ACADEMY AWARD WINNER BEST ACTOR, RAMI MALEK played the role of FREDDY MERCURY and did an outstanding performance. The drummer in the real QUEEN, ROGER TAYLOR, wasn't portrayed correctly in the movie. I encountered ROGER TAYLOR a few evenings in LAHAINA, MAUI, HAWAII, during the band's peak, and he had a big ego which was justified because of their enormous popularity, not a good impression.

"THE BODYGUARD" as the saying goes, "Life is only six degrees of separation." THE BODYGUARD is applied to this saying. I attended a private exclusive birthday at "THE MARY PICKFORD ESTATE" where some of the scenes in the movie were shot. The security attended the party with three checkpoints. MARVIN DAVIS had a circus tent with a river running through the dining area, and RALPH WAITE who owned a business similar to my business was also the host of AA meetings that I attended to give support to a loved one. As RALPH WAITE ate at my establishment, I asked him about working with WHITNEY HOUSTON in "THE BODYGUARD." He said, "WHITNEY HOUSTON is a SUPERSTAR with all the world at her disposal and no limitations of her career." To me, she's a beautiful woman, one of the greatest singers of all time, and she's someone taken away too early with bad choices.

"THE GRADUATE" is one of music's greatest duos, songwriters, and harmonies second to none. And a list of our most memorable tunes from "THE GRADUATE" are "MRS. ROBINSON," "THE SOUND OF SILENCE," "SCARBOROUGH FAIR/CANTICLE," "APRIL

COME SHE WILL," and all these songs that are relevant today. And they continued to produce many hits into the '70s. BUCK HENRY and CALDER WILLINGHAM co-wrote the movie. BUCK HENRY had his cameo as the front desk hotel employee when BENJAMIN BRADDOCK, DUSTIN HOFFMAN were asking for a room. Years earlier, I ran into DUSTIN HOFFMAN in LAHAINA, MAUI, HAWAII. When I surprisingly approached him, I startled him at first by whispering in his ears. "PLASTIC, PLASTIC, THE FUTURE OS PLASTIC, AND LOOK WHAT I AM DOING NOW." HOFFMAN laughed, and we ran across each other for the next few days. One of the greatest duos in music.

"HAROLD AND MAUDE." This iconic and memorable movie was filmed in the bay area cities of PALO ALTO/STANFORD, WOODSIDE, MENLO PARK, SOUTH SAN FRANCISCO, EMERYVILLE (before it was EMERYVILLE) and the coastline.

The locations of the shooting of the movie were ST. ANN'S CATHOLIC church in PALO ALTO, back cycling streets in the hills of STANFORD UNIVERSITY, THE NATIONAL CEMETERY in MILLBRAE, the bank in BURLINGAME, woods of WOODSIDE, the dump is now where GOOGLE HEADQUARTERS is located, and the residence was the FOLGER (Coffee)ESTATE in Woodside, California. ALMA SPRECKLES owned. ALMA SPRECKLES also built and bankrolled the PALACE of FINE ARTS in the SAN FRANCISCO MARINA DISTRICT. The old 1920 iconic bath beach house foundation, and PALO ALTO MILITARY ACADEMY. GREAT to reflect on these historical sites.

The thought of dating MAUDE (RUTH GORDON) who was anticipating her eightieth birthday and a young man, HAROLD, was fascinated by this older woman that he fell in love with her.

Most importantly, the movie introduced us to the music of CAT STEVENS, now known as YUSAF ISLAM. At one time, PRESIDENT GEORGE BSUH banned YUSAF ISLAM from being a MUSLIM and felt he was a threat. His crusade was to build rehabilitation centers for the youth of EUROPE. Eventually, the banned was lifted, he then performed at his INDUCTION to THE ROCK and ROLL HALL OF FAME.

"FOOTLOOSE," "CADDYSHACK," "TOP GUN," "WINNIE THE POOH," and the masterpiece "LEAP OF FAITH." These guys produced an introduction album called "SITTIN IN" which introduced us to "LOGGINS and MESSINA." The songs included in these movies were produced by "KENNY LOGGINS" after he took a hiatus from "JIM MESSINA" who was in another All-STAR supergroup called POCO.

I first met JIM MESSINA in a bar on STATE STREET in SANTA BARBARA in the late '70s. Everyone was having a wild time, and I caught the eye of a young woman. We turned to each, and he said, "She won't be happy with me checking out other women" as his girlfriend approached.

They released a series of albums that were well received and got plenty of air time. Then KENNY LOGGINS decided to pursue a solo career.

MOVIE SOUNDTRACKS that made him an even bigger star and a series of CDs including "RETURN TO POOH CORNER," lullabies for children and the most transitional CD in his career, "LEAP OF FAITH." And one of my top ten ALBUMS/CDs of all time.

I have seen LOGGINS and MESSINA, and KENNY LOGGINS concerts at least twenty-plus times. The most memorable, "LOGGINS and MESSINA" concert was in SANTA BARBARA bowl at their reunion concert. I sat directly behind the wives, children, and friends. The band was fabulous, but "LOGGINS and MESSINA" were well reserved due to not wanting to look different to their entourage. It was the first concert I walked out of before it was finished.

KENNY LOGGINS has seven million followers and at seventy-five-plus is a visionary in music. Hopefully, you saw these movies! Rent them!

"PITCH PERFECT" is a series of movies, three that had octopelio women singers. HANA MAE LEE was the girlfriend of my close lawyer friend's son. She was "A BREATH OF FRESH AIR!"

WEST SIDE STORY. My mother took my sister and I to the movie in PHILADELPHIA, PENNSYLVANIA.

Mom had seen the BROADWAY PLAY in NEW YORK earlier. So she wanted to also do the shopping with the two of us. So we boarded a train to PHILADELPHIA.

We arrived finally at the movie theater. In those days, they had ushers who would walk you down to seats available using a flashlight.

My mother gave a directive to come and retrieve us before the closing scenes of the movie due to the dramatic and saddening ending.

TONIGHT, MARIA, THE JETS, LEONARD BERNSTEIN, NATALIE WOOD, years later, I would do a magazine shoot with ROBERT WAGNER, who was with NATALIE on that fateful night on the boat at CATALINA. RITA MORENO, TEN OSCARS, almost as many as BEN HUR. MIKLOS ROZSA to his credits, EL CID, KING OF KINGS, JUNGLE BOOK, THE THIEF OF BAGDAD, THE LOST WEEKEND, to name a few.

DAN FOGELBERG

My top three favorite artists!

I was introduced to his music by a friend in SANTA CRUZ. Once I heard his first album, I was hooked, line, and sinker.

He recorded his albums in a remote part of COLORADO outside of BOULDER. The studio was a frequent recording spot for CHICAGO, and many other artists.

CARIBOU RANCH in NEDERLAND, COLORADO. MICHAEL JACKSON, JOE WALSH, BILLY JOEL, JOHN LENNON, STEVIE NICKS, and ELTON JOHN were some of the artists who recorded until it closed after fifteen years. It was located around the corner from my favorite snowboarding ski area, EL DORA.

FOGELBERG collaborated and produced songs with so many artists. His songwriting is my BIBLE for your soul, and compassion for music!

I remember being in a boutique in SAN FRANCISCO walking around with my SONY WALKMAN singing along to my DAN FOGELBERG music when a woman tapped me on the shoulder and asked, "Are you a fan of DAN FOGELBERG?" I said, "Am I singing too loud?" And she said I am married to DAN FOGELBERG, I AM MAGGIE SLAYMAKER.

One afternoon getting ready to close my business, a young woman came knocking on my locked business door. She was persistent and would not stop. She could see me in the window opening in the back as I opened the door, she asked if I was Randy? And I answered Yes! The next thing, she started crying. I noticed she had children in her car. So I inquired, "Are you all right?"

She told me that she was the illegitimate daughter of DAN FOGELBERG! I said, "What?" People who frequented my business knew I was a big fan of the late FOGELBERG! He passed away, on my birthday, and he's way too young!

Anyway, the woman was asking for a game plan to approach DAN FOGELBERG'S agent and family. She said her mother on her deathbed with cancer, told her she had a one-night stand with DAN FOGELBERG and that she was his daughter.

She even had the same facial features! I flat out asked her if she had an agenda, mainly financial, and she denied it! Her attorney contacted me, and I said, "This inquiry should be with FOGELBERG'S family and business manager." I never responded to their inquiries.

COACHELLA and STAGECOACH MUSIC FESTIVALS

I entertained the founders of these events in the beginning when they were getting the FESTIVALS off the ground.

I sold my business where I spent half of my life to the CFO of the music festivals.

You can operate the world's most successful music venues with 2,400 concerts and events and thousands of employees.

Operating a small business with a few employees has its challenges where you need to communicate and be responsible for monitoring your business. You need to build a base and foundation.

The festivals returned after a pandemic break.

SEAL

I returned to the desert one hot afternoon after traveling the globe for seven weeks on the tennis and golf tours.

My ex-wife talked me into venturing to CHILE to do some summer skiing and snowboarding. We left PALM DESERT on a warm 122-degree day and arrived in SANTIAGO, CHILE, early in the morning.

The CAPTAIN of the CHILE DAVIS CUP team picked us up at the airport, and we drove to PORTILLO SKI RESORT. Our car was the first allowed through the mountain checkpoint since it snowed six feet the night before.

As we drove above the timberline and had numerous thoughts on the plane the night before about the book "ALIVE," we arrived at the ski resort. That was our airplane cabin movie to CHILE about a plane crashing into the ANDES and survival horrific stories.

Anyway, it was breathtaking. It was -22 degrees and chill factor -40 in twenty-four hours that was a 162 degrees difference! Think about that.

The fresh snow was great! The resort had piped-in music on its slopes! After a while, the "SPANISH" and "SOUTH AMERICAN" music finally got to me. As I sat down to eat lunch, a tune came on. The BEACH BOYS, CALIFORNIA GIRLS, which is like an anthem to beach-going CALIFORNIANS like myself. I know every word and verse!

I belted out the first verse and then out of nowhere, a man of color started singing along with me. He even sang the second verse hitting a wide range of notes. He gave me the thumbs up and said, "YOU GOT A GOOD VOICE."

I said to him as he was leaving, "You're SEAL?" He made a thumbs up and a wink as he left.

During the BNP Tennis tournament in INDIAN WELLS, SEAL attended the matches since he had his good buddy playing. I saw SEAL amongst all the "autograph seekers" and worked my way in to say hi! I said, "Do you remember skiing in CHILE last summer and singing?" SEAL interrupted me and said, "BEACH BOYS, CALIFORNIA GIRLS," and started to sing. I let him know I live in the desert!

TIDBIT STORIES

BEACH BOYS, BEATLES, JERRY GARCIA, BILL GRAHAM, BOB MARLEY, GIL SCOTT HERON, "PITCH PERFECT," JESSE COLIN YOUNG and THE YOUNGBLOODS, WARREN ZEVON, JOHNNY MATHIS, NAT KING COLE, QUEEN (ROGER TAYLOR), BILL CHAMPLIN (SONS OF CHAMPLIN), JOHN DENVER, BARRY GORDON, ERIC BURDON and THE ANIMALS, ELO and JEFF LYNNE.

GIL SCOTT HERON, "THE REVOLUTION" and "AIN'T NO THING AS SUPERMAN." My buddy asked me if I wanted to go to this jazz club to hear a GREAT sax player. UNBELIEVABLE, the first RAP song before there was rap. A visionary of what the future may bring.

BOB MARLEY and THE WAILERS I saw in MAUI, HAWAII, under the warmth of the stars and the breeze of the ocean. The following day, my buddy and I were flying back to the mainland, CALIFORNIA. The flight attendant approached us about the empty seat between us and asked if we would mind having a twelve-year-old sit between us on the flight to CALIFORNIA. "Sure, no problem." This young man was ZIGGY MARLEY, BOB MARLEY'S son. A few months later, we went to one of BOB MARLEY'S final concerts at the SANTA BARBARA bowl. What a GREAT venue. BOB MARLEY was sick and passed away in 1981. "RASTA EVERY LIVING, RASTA THE FIRST."

"THE BEATLES." My brother returned from ENGLAND in 1962 with an album he picked from a group who was taking the music scene in ENGLAND. The album was "THE BEATLES" with the young fab-four on the cover.

I wore out this album on my bedroom stereo. My neighbor buddies who loved music would hang out in my room singing along with the tunes. We listened to the album so many times that we knew every word!

So we had "SHOW and TELL" every Wednesday, and the four of us asked our teacher that we had a special "SHOW and TELL." The BEATLES had yet to be discovered and would perform on the ED SULLIVAN SHOW three months later.

So I brought my little record player, put on "THE BEATLES," and lip-synched to all the sounds and played "air guitar, drums, etc." By lunchtime, we were the talk of our school.

We were asked to perform in the general assembly in the auditorium the following week, so I had an ingenious idea to provide a program and charge for it. We made money!

Three months later, "THE BEATLES" performed for the USA on THE ED SULLIVAN, and the rest was history.

A few years later, my mother acquired tickets to "THE BEATLES" in BALTIMORE, MARYLAND. My mother was involved with politics in MARYLAND that she got special perks! My sister screamed for almost two hours.

"JERRY GARCIA" of "THE GRATEFUL DEAD" lived and played throughout the bay area. Some of the members of the band attended PALO ALTO HIGH SCHOOL (see PALO ALTO HIGH SCHOOL).

My cousin worked with "BILL GRAHAM" and "THE FILLMORE WEST" in SAN FRANCISCO, CALIFORNIA. My cousin owned "CRYSTAL SHIP LIGHT COMPANY" who performed all the light shows, and special effects (they were not called that in those days) but did whatever was necessary for your drug-induced experience to be a good one!

He formed a bond with JERRY GARCIA and a friendship like brothers. He became "GRATEFUL DEADS" and JERRY GARCIA'S confident advisor. He also was very close with "GRACE SLICK" who lived in PALO ALTO who also attended PALO ALTO HIGH and CASTILLEJA.

JERRY GARCIA was the best man at my cousin's wedding. The two of them promoted and delivered concerts second to none in the bay area during that time. I even met JERRY GARCIA and spoke to him for about thirty minutes. I was a high school student. We talked about the week before me playing a lacrosse game at the same venue where the concert venue was across the street from STANFORD SHOPPING CENTER.

My cousin was devastated when JERRY GARCIA died. "BILL GRAHAM" died a few years later. My cousin's posters are collectibles that are worth big bucks. He created most of the posters for all of FILLMORE WEST.

My neighbor discovered and signed NAT KING COLE to all his recording deals. Whenever NAT KING COLE had a number one hit, DAN, my neighbor, would buy a ranch. He has five ranches outside of Chicago. Dan is ninety-four years of youth, he also shared when NATALIE COLE came to perform in the desert, she was narcissistic and didn't give him the time of day! Even though he produced five top one hits.

I worked in a popular restaurant in MAUI, HAWAII. We had lots of guests from all walks of life. ROGER TAYLOR of QUEEN would frequent the restaurant when in the ISLANDS. QUEEN was on top of their game. I went over and said hi, and he didn't want to acknowledge a low-life good-looking tan waiter.

My roommate in MAUI, HAWAII, had the only ROCK AND ROLL band on the ISLAND. The band was always busy. I would occasionally sing a song or two if I was in the area they were playing. The bass guitarist was the caretaker of a few members of FLEETWOOD MAC'S home where WARREN ZEVON spent some time. My roommate's band was playing at an OUTRIGGER event and we were joined on stage for a few songs.

I was arriving to work, and we had a stage where we had live music, and it opened at 9:00 p.m. I kept hearing tunes that were familiar to me. I was told the band was practicing for the evening's performance so I ventured down and said, "The music sounds like THE SONS OF CHAMPLIN" who I have seen a few times in NOR-CAL. Sure enough, it was BILL CHAMPLIN doing a sound check. He was impressed that I knew his music and from NOR-CAL. We had a great conversation. A few months later, he joined the group CHICAGO and added a new dimension to their sound. He helped CHICAGO be relevant for years. I even shared with him that our hostess was married to TINY TIM of "TIPTOE THROUGH THE TULIPS."

JOHN DENVER of ASPEN, COLORADO. I participated at GERALD FORD INVITATIONAL. Part of the festivities was an outdoor concert at VAIL PARK. The venue was an amphitheater with the stage area that was covered and assigned seating for two hundred safely covered and one thousand in the amphitheater area. There were other musical stars who would only do three songs. JOHN DENVER was having a rollercoaster life happening: divorce, DUIs, and differences about environmental issues. I ONLY wanted to see him perform, he came onto the stage on the EAGLE VAIL RIVER and thunderous, lightning in the distance, and started singing "ROCKY MOUNTAIN HIGH." It was the most memorable performance I ever saw. The weather contributed a lot. I was in the covered area where the weather did not interrupt his three-song performance. He sang "ANNIE'S SONG" even though he was going through a divorce, then "CALYPSO," that was it. A few months later, he died of an unfortunate flying accident.

ERIC BURDON lived in the desert and was a frequent visitor to my business. I was introduced to him by MING LOWE who is an artist and a photographer whose works have been shown throughout the world. She was a close friend to many of the top musicians. ERIC was a constant companion when they visited me.

One day, ERIC came in and was listening to my assortment of CDs. I always played one CD, "THE WONDER YEARS" box set that featured music from the television series and an ERIC BURDON song in the music track.

He asked to see the box "THE WONDER YEARS," and immediately called his business manager. I asked him to look into the royalties contract from this CD set. The next time, ERIC BURDON told me he was given back royalties fees!

Do you know ERIC BURDON did not receive really any type of royalties for the "HOUSE of the RISING SUN?" He learned from his mistake of not signing contracts early in his career accordingly.

He had future hits with "WAR" as the front man. "SPILL THE WINE" then he moved on.

He formed a "SUPERGROUP" of various musicians to carry on his legacy and the band members songs.

ERIC had some health issues from partying hard, riding a HARLEY DAVIDSON motorcycle, and making changes in his life. His new wife became his manager and confidant and put him on to a healthy lifestyle.

The last time I saw ERIC BURDON was at the COSTCO in Palm Desert in the sample line of food stations. We talked and had a good laugh. He now resides in the Ojai area of California.

JEFF LYNNE was the GREATEST music engineer of producing albums, CDs from GEORGE HARRISON "ALL THINGS MUST PASS," TOM PETTY, PAUL McCARTNEY. JEFF LYNNE was considered the fifth BEATLE.

E.L.O. and later the "TRAVELING WILBURYS" with the late ROY ORBISON, his best friend, the late GEORGE HARRISON, the late TOM PETTY, and the iconic BOB DYLAN, and he was the fifth member.

JEFF LYNNE's home in ENGLAND had everything, even the bathrooms were studios to create different sounds. JEFF LYNNE is a GENIUS and PERFECTIONIST. See his show at WIMBLEY with E.L.O., a documentary on HBO!

His manager, CRAIG FRUIN, who handles the biggest names in music, contacted me to investigate an impostor in our area who was picking up women and telling them he was JEFF LYNNE. I was ecstatic to assist and assist in getting this impostor caught. Big E.L.O. fan!

CONCERT'S I'VE ATTENDED

I PERSONALLY MET THEM—CONVERSATION—$ WORTH IT
THE BEATLES, CAT STEVENS (YUSAF ISLAM) $, WILLIE NELSON, CHICAGO & SONS OF CHAMPLIN (**BILL CHAMPLIN), SLY and THE FAMILY STONE, **TIM HARDIN, ELVIN BISHOP (*MICKEY THOMAS), BOB MARLEY (**ZIGGY MARLEY), JOHN DENVER, WRECKING CREW (** GLEN CAMPBELL, **HAL BLAINE), SAGA (**MICHAEL SADLER, **IAN CRICHTON, **JIM CRISHTON) $, HOT TUNA (**PAPA JOHN CREECH), **LOUIS "SATCHMO" ARMSTRONG, **WARREN ZEVON, HEART, JOSE FELICIANO, MOODY BLUES (** JUSTIN HAYWARD, **JOHN LODGE, **GRAEME EDGE, 15 X's) $, ELO & TRAVELING WILBURYS (**JEFF LYNNE) *BOB DYLAN, *TOM PETTY, CHARLIE DANIELS, CREDENCE CLEARWATER, REVIVAL $, PABLO CRUISE (**CORY LERIOS, **DAVID JENKINS, **STEVE PRICE) $, CANNED HEAT, DONOVAN, **RICHIE HAVENS, HAIR, PITCH PERFECT (** HANA MAE LEE), THE UNSINKABLE MOLLY BROWN, LONDON, ENGLAND, DEBBIE REYNOLDS $, NUTCRACKER SUITE, OPERA HOUSE, SAN FRANCISCO, CALIFORNIA (6's) $, JOEY BONAMASSA, VIENNA OPERA HOUSE $, JESUS CHRIST SUPERSTAR (**CARL ANDERSON, JUDAS) $, **MUSIC FROM THE HEART, McCALLUM THEATRE, PALM DESERT, RANDY McWILLIAMS $, CONCERT'S AT VARIOUS PARK'S THROUGHOUT THE WORLD, REDROCKS AMPHITHEATER, COLORADO, $, MUSIC OF HEAVENS, BASILICA of SANTA MARIA del POPOLO, ROME, ITALY $, STEVIE WONDER $, *VIC DAMONE, *DINAH CARROLL, I PERFORMED ON STAGE FOR THEM, SMOOTHER'S BROTHERS (**BOTH), *JONI MITCHELL, **BOB HOPE, **GINGER RODGERS, **FRANK SINATRA, **FRANK DAMANTE, **BARBARA SINATRA, **DINAH SHORE, **JOAN BAEZ, LYDIA PENCE & COLD BLOOD, **COUNTRY JOE McDONALD, WAR & ERIC BURDON and THE ANIMALS (**ERIC BURDON) $, RONNIE LANE, ERIC CLAPTON $, JOURNEY, **BOZ SCAGGS $, *JACKSON BROWN $, *DAN FOGELBERG, JOE COCKER, JEFF BECK $, FACES, ROD STEWART $, BAD COMPANY, PAUL RODGERS $, JIMMY PAIGE, **THE ROMERO'S, KANSAS (**ROBBY STENHARDT, GRATEFUL DEAD (** JERRY GARCIA), JEFFERSON AIRPLANE & JEFFERSON STARSHIP (**MICKEY THOMAS, **GRACE SLICK) $, SPIRIT, QUICKSILVER MESSENGER SERVICE, CSN & Y, CROSBY & NASH (**DAVID CROSBY, **NEIL YOUNG) $, AMERICA (** DEWEY BUNNELL, **GERRY BECKLEY) $, BEACH BOY'S (*BRIAN WILSON, DENNIS WILSON, BRUCE JOHNSTON), EAGLES, RUSH (* GEDDY LEE, *NEIL PEARL), **WEIRD AL, JOY OF COOKING, **TINY TIM, KINGSTON TRIO (**BOB SHANE), CHARLIE WATTS, BILL WYMAN, HIROSHIMA, ELECTRIC FLAG, ELTON JOHN, MICHAEL JACKSON, COMMODORES, **AL GREEN, LIONEL RITCHEY, GEORGE BENSON, JANIS JOPLIN & THE HOLDING COMPANY, GIL SCOTT HERON, STEVE MILLER, HUEY LEWIS & THE NEWS $, PAT METHENY $, ROBERT PALMER, LINDA RONSTADT, DOOBIE BROTHERS (*PATRICK SIMMONS), **MICHAEL McDONALD $, JAMES TAYLOR $, JIMMY WEBB, HALL & OATES $, HENRY MANCINI, IRON BUTTERFLY, IT'S A BEAUTIFUL DAY, EARTH, WIND, & FIRE $, CHAMBER'S BROTHERS, CHRISTOPHER CROSS $, BRUCE HORNSBY $, LOGGINS & MESSINA $ (*JIM MESSINA), KENNY LOGGINS $, FLEETWOOD MAC $ (**STEVIE NICKS, **LINDSEY BUCKINGHAM) **STEVIE NICKS.

TENNIS

This chapter will try to have content chronically from respecting past experiences of champions to today's stars.

* I have been humbled, blessed, lucky, and fortunate to be given the opportunity to coach and train tennis clinics, chef, and mentor of HALL OF FAME, GRAND SLAM CHAMPIONS (collectively one hundred Grand Slam Championships), ATP AND WTA CHAMPIONS, DAVIS AND FED CUP, NCAA CHAMPIONS. (Pictured "MOIS" ROLAND GARROS, PARIS, FRANCE)

ROD "ROCKET" LAVER

The "GREATEST" tennis player of ALL-TIME is ROD LAVER. The winner of two "GRAND SLAMS" which is the four-tennis majors in a single calendar year. SLAM DUNK! No one in my lifetime will ever do that!

AUSTRALIAN OPEN, (MELBOURNE, AUSTRALIA), FRENCH OPEN (ROLAND GARROS, PARIS, FRANCE), WIMBLEDON (WIMBLEDON, ENGLAND) and U.S. OPEN (NEW YORK).

These tournaments were played on different surfaces. AUSTRALIAN OPEN (grass courts), FRENCH OPEN (red clay courts), WIMBLEDON (grass courts), and U.S. OPEN (grass courts).

Think about it not only winning two GRAND SLAMS in 1962 and 1969. In 1959 and 1960, "ROCKET" won WIMBLEDON, and in 1961, he won FRENCH OPEN MIXED DOUBLES titles. Then in 1959, 1960, and 1961, "ROCKET" won AUSTRALIAN DOUBLES OPEN titles and another in 1969, including WIMBLEDON DOUBLES in 1971.

Then in 1960, "ROCKET" won his first singles GRAND SLAM titles in his home country of AUSTRALIA on grass, won WIMBLEDON GENTLEMEN SINGLES in 1961, and the following year 1962, he won his first of two GRAND SLAMS sweeps, AUSTRALIAN OPEN, FRENCH OPEN, WIMBLEDON GENTLEMEN'S CHAMPIONSHIP, and U.S. OPEN, and repeated this again in 1969. "ROCKET" won the WIMBLEDON GENTLEMEN'S CHAMPIONSHIPS in 1968.

Let's add all of this up: TWENTY GRAND SLAM TITLES! MIXED DOUBLES, DOUBLES, and SINGLES CHAMPIONSHIPS. Two GRAND SLAM TITLES and only one other male player has almost pulled it off in 2021: NOVAK! "ROCKET" is my GOAT, and he's a terrific person!

ROD LAVER found this court formula successful being a native AUSTRALIAN. He learned tennis on grass courts. At that time, three-to-four majors were played on grass! "ROCKET" as he was known, won two SLAMS over a seven-year-time period.

At this time, professional tennis was non-existent until players decided to organize and set up a professional tour. "ROCKET" and some of the greats (read more in this chapter) made the reality of playing for prize money.

As years progressed on the tour, the surfaces changed for the majors: AUSTRALIAN OPEN (hardcourts), FRENCH OPEN (Roland Garros, red brick clay), and U.S. OPEN (hardcourts). The only surface that did not change was WIMBLEDON (grass). The dynamic of the majors changed drastically.

Let's get back to the "ROCKETMAN," ROD LAVER.

I was fortunate to get to know this legendary, HALL OF FAME, the "WORLD'S GREATEST PLAYER." He lived in PALM DESERT, RANCHO MIRAGE, where I operated my businesses.

We first met at MISSION HILLS COUNTRY CLUB where I worked during a tennis week with HALL OF FAME players. ROD LAVER, RON HOLMBERG, PANCHO GONZALEZ, VIC SEIXAS, FRED KOVALESKI, DENNIS RALSTON, MARTY RIESSEN, TOM GORMAN, PANCHO SEGURA, JOSE HIGUERAS, and others.

Throughout the following years, we would cross paths since we were neighbors who lived a few miles apart.

One morning, I went to our local grocery store. As I left the store, I saw someone with their head in the trash can rummaging through the contents of the trash can. Newspapers were being examined and then tossed by this individual in the air! As I looked closer, it was ROD LAVER'S head and throwing papers from the trash can!

I said, "ROCKET what are you doing?" He said, "I'm sitting here at the "coffee/donut" shop and reading a paper that was left, and then the continuance of article I was reading was not there. So I even went to buy a paper to finish the article, but the store was sold out, so I resorted to my last option, digging in the trash can."

Think about that, visually, with the world's "GREATEST TENNIS PLAYER OF ALL-TIME," the "GOAT."

I worked with some clients at his club and would run into him often. He was always friendly and cordial. He was always inquired by players visiting me to train, and if they would like to hit balls with the "ROCKET." Imagine when I said to the players I was working with, "Heh, do you want to hit some balls with ROD LAVER?" Everyone jumped.

If I was having lunch at the tennis clubhouse, he would always come over and say hello! Class act.

Eventually, he had some health issues that he had to address, and decided to move to the beach and seriously took up playing golf as much as he could. "ROCKET" is as strong as ever in 2022.

"MOIS" CENTER COURT ROLAND GARROS, PARIS

BILL TILDEN

Lots of things have been written both negative and positive about this "HALL OF FAME" player from the 1920s.

BILL TILDEN won the WIMBLEDON singles championship in 1920 and 1921. He won UNITED STATES OPEN single championships from 1920 to 1925. He won UNITED STATES OPEN single championship in 1928. He won WIMBLEDON, UNITED STATES doubles championship in 1927.

He was controversial in his private life, and that was made public. There were many accusations that were disturbing to all tennis fans (like MICHAEL JACKSON). BILL TILDEN had to live with these claims throughout his career. Discuss that later.

The roaring twenties! Tennis player's attire was truly a fashion statement where men wore long white slacks, long/short sleeve shirts, dress shoes, (the infancy of tennis shoes) and tennis shoes. Men were dressed extremely well and were easily fit into a club scene to just walk off the court to the clubhouse for a brewski/cocktail. Tennis was an elitist social class during this time and for many years to come.

BILL TILDEN was a slender, athletic, handsome, and VERY competitive man!

BILL TILDEN was a marked man! Rumor had it that he enjoyed the company of young boys or young men. He had to deal with these accusations everywhere that he went or played a tournament!

BILL TILDEN was unbeatable in the twenties at the UNITED STATES OPEN as a singles champion. SIX UNITED STATES OPEN

SINGLES CHAMPIONSHIPS, ONE DOUBLES UNITED STATES CHAMPIONSHIP, and TWO WIMBLEDON GENTLEMEN SINGLES CHAMPIONSHIPS. BILL TILDEN was the "GOAT" of grass-court championships from 1920–1925!

He would have won more titles if he had embraced traveling by ocean liner to AUSTRALIA and if he decided to travel to FRANCE for the FRENCH OPEN. TILDEN did not want to stay in EUROPE from FRENCH OPEN to GENTLEMEN'S CHAMPIONSHIPS AT WIMBLEDON.

So let me address the accusations made about BILL TILDEN being basically a pedophile" for his fondness of little boys!

My client had the opportunity to outbid the ITF, HALL of FAME, and USTA at auction for the "PERPETUAL TROPHY," BILL TILDEN'S personal diaries, and other tennis historic memorabilia.

Let's talk about the "PERPETUAL TROPHY." This trophy, pictured with me is the most famous trophy in tennis history. My client casually has this trophy placed on a "conversation" coffee table in his home.

BILL TILDEN was fed up with the constant accusations of his personal life. Back in the day at tournaments, if you lost your match, the following day, you would be assigned to be a line judge in the next day's match. Think about that. Can you imagine today having SAMPRAS, EDBERG, and NOVAK being a linesperson after they lost a match the previous day at a GRAND SLAM? That was the protocol of tournament play then!

So in the finals of the UNITED STATES SINGLES OPEN CHAMPIONSHIPS in 1928, the "PERPETUAL TROPHY" was placed and situated on the top of the table to be given to the winner of the CHAMPIONSHIP. BILL TILDEN was fed up with the accusations, the bad line calls his competitors were making in the tournament, and favoring his opponent.

BILL TILDEN was serving for the match in the finals of the UNITED STATES OPEN. He took the four balls in play on court (that has changed throughout the years, more today) in his left hand, and served four straight aces; and directly be-lined his court exit to the "PERPETUAL TROPHY" table, grabbed the trophy, and walked off with it under his arm! The trophy was not SEEN again till 1979! Yes, 1979!

The "PERPETUAL TROPHY," the great mystery of its whereabouts finally appeared in 1979. A woman friend of BILL TILDEN'S had kept the trophy in a safe space in her home.

The "PERPETUAL TROPHY" and BILL TILDEN'S personal items were auctioned off—his entire daily diary collection of twenty years, which included his playing days of the 1920s! BILL TILDEN'S PERSONAL DIARIES!

I spent an entire week at my client's residence in LEXINGTON, KENTUCKY, reading as many of BILL TILDEN'S diaries as I could. Over the next few years at my client's homes in COLORADO, KENTUCKY, I would totally be immersed in reading ALL of BILL TILDEN'S diaries.

My client outbid the most infamous tennis organizations in the world to privately own pieces of tennis history! My conclusion to NO TIME did BILL TILDEN from his own words in the diaries ever mentioned any "pedophile behavior." He had a love of youth and those less fortunate! I often thought about the strange actions of MICHAEL JACKSON and his accusations. JACKSON slept with children. BILL TILDEN NEVER did that, he was completely vindicated of any wrongdoing in my book!

The picture is of "PERPETUAL TROPHY" along with numerous other famous and world's largest championship trophy. THE DAVIS CUP TROPHY in PARIS, FRANCE!

(TOP/L-R) DAVIS CUP, PARIS – NHL STANLEY CUP, TORONTO – IOS PERPETUAL TROPHY, LEXINGTON – NHL HALL OF FAME, TORONTO – CALIFORNIA GOVERNOR FITNESS

BOBBY RIGGS

Probably the most famous tennis player in the history of the sport. A defeat led to a movement in ALL of women's sports like no other. At the time, he was the GREATEST television viewing audience of seventy million plus!

BOBBY RIGGS changed sporting events forever!

Additionally, this event was the start of introducing side shows, and future Super Bowl events. The marketing of an event.

BOBBY RIGGS won six major tennis events in a three-year window from MIXED DOUBLES, DOUBLES, and SINGLES major championships.

Most importantly, he knew he could make some money going after the women's tennis game. He challenged the stature of the women's game and especially challenged MARGARET COURT, the winner of more majors than anyone. Remember this was in the '70s before the future of women's games revolutionized in the nineties!

THE "BATTLE OF THE SEXES" in 1973!

I spent time with BOBBY RIGGS in MONTECITO, CALIFORNIA, during a CHAMPIONS tennis event.

I was involved with almost every characteristic of the tournament. I was the GODFATHER to former "BIG SERVE" tennis major champion ROSCOE TANNER.

It was decided that all the alcohol would be stored in my suite at the BILTMORE in SANTA BARBARA. The reason was that I did not consume alcohol, and there would be no issues to stock the various bars at the event.

Little did I know my consistent visitors to my suite nightly would be ROSCOE TANNER and BOBBY RIGGS. It was like clockwork with a knock on the door at about midnight, 1:00 a.m. for them to continue their drinking. I would sit up in my bed and be entertained by these two.

What was talked about nightly was "BATTLE OF THE SEXES." BOBBY RIGGS explained that he made more money betting on himself to lose than to win! The match was fixed by BOBBY RIGGS. BOBBY RIGGS was a big gambler and a heavy drinker. BOBBY RIGGS "BATTLE OF THE SEXES," and he NEVER changed his story!

One morning at the tournament site, MONTECITO POLO CLUB, BOBBY RIGGS and I hit some balls for about an hour. At one point, he decided to make our hitting session a bit more challenging by incorporating the placement of a chair on his side of the court.

He would return my shot, run to the chair to sit down, get up quickly and move to the ball. I had just hit to his side of the court. We did this for thirty minutes to the delight of those laughing and watching. An amazing player, with memories of a lifetime!

What hit home with me is he was in his seventies, and still had that spark.

I ran into BOBBY again at the L.A. OPEN at UCLA tennis center where he was watching my players playing doubles the #1 doubles team in the world.

Unfortunately, he was consumed with his alcoholic ways which led to his demise a few years later. Unfortunately, he did not see the better lifestyle at the end of the tunnel.

ROSCOE "BIG SERVE" TANNER

I traveled, worked, and became the godfather to ROSCOE'S daughter. Our relationship abruptly ended after seven years.

I have decided to take the high road. I have compassion for someone who made some LIFE-CHANGING major BAD decisions!

The old saying applies to ROSCOE TANNER, "Be nice to the people on the way up because you might see them again on the way down."

In 1979, ROSCOE TANNER recorded the fastest serve in tennis, 153 M.P.H. against RAUL RAMIREZ at the PILOT PEN TOURNAMENT, which would eventually become the BNP in INDIAN WELLS, CALIFORNIA.

Remember I am taking the high road of ROSCOE TANNER who was a STANFORD INDIAN superstar under HALL OF FAME coach DICK GOULD and the winningest coach in NCAA history!

(Refer to story of COACH JOHN WOODEN, MISS USA PAGEANT, and CELEBRITY chapter 5!)

From the beginning, how our paths crossed, and an interesting friendship developed.

I met ROSCOE TANNER by accident when he was doing laundry at a local laundromat that was across the street from my business.

ROSCOE came into my small restaurant to have breakfast, waiting for his clothes to dry while his clothes were going through the drying cycle.

There were some articles in frames on my business walls that referred to my other business. At the time, I was working with a future "HALL OF FAME" baseball player, a professional PGA golfer who was the first NCAA golfer to be a four-time ALL-AMERICAN, a woman who was the body double for JACQUELIN BASSET, and a few upcoming professional tennis players.

Our personalities and my athletic background were an instant connection. Additionally, a trainer (unheard of at that time) who rises to the challenges in sports, yoga, stretching, weights, plyometrics (not the traditional), cardiovascular, aqua therapy, nutritionist (that was complementary to your diet), chef, injury prevention, etc.!

My focus and success were preparing you for your athletic challenges. Most of the techniques I incorporated were never heard of, and EVERYONE is doing them today.

As "NATIONAL SPORTSWRITER OF THE YEAR," THOMAS BONK of *L.A. TIMES* said about me in LA's print, "I was the guru of tennis at the time."

ROSCOE TANNER just had reconstructive surgery on his famous serving arm. ROSCOE was a lefty, and he had a unique service motion of hitting the service toss on the way up. The late VIC BRADEN, a tennis instructor, made a lot of money teaching ROSCOE's service motion.

ROSCOE was 5'10" 190 lbs., and strong.

ROSCOE TANNER was a STANFORD UNIVERSITY tennis player. At the time when he played the PACIFIC ATHLETIC CONFERENCE, he was called the "PAC-8."

According to ROSCOE, the first player team meeting with the future "HALL OF FAME" coach, DICK GOULD (who amassed seventeen NCAA team titles at STANFORD) had written on the chalkboard the upcoming season matches in the "PAC-8." COACH circled the opponents they should win against and the teams they will lose to.

ROSCOE raised his voice and asked coach, "Why are you predicting we will lose to USC and UCLA?" "Let's change that, COACH!" COACH had NEVER had a player with that much confidence and to have an attitude, "We are NOT going to lose to USC, UCLA, COACH!" "Let's go!" This is what ROSCOE TANNER told me on what transpired that day.

ROSCOE had some success on the new ATP professional tour. In 1977, he won the AUSTRALIAN OPEN. That was the year AUSTRALIAN OPEN was played twice within a six-month window.

The infancy tour wanted to have the AUSTRALIAN OPEN be played in January. The surface continued to be grass (hard court today) which was advantageous for a big server as ROSCOE TANNER.

ROSCOE career titles were thirteen singles titles, fifteen doubles titles, and AUSTRALIAN OPEN CHAMPION, grass 1977.

When we first got together, he was interested in my training/coaching/nutrition techniques. At the time, NO one was doing what I was doing.

ROSCOE just had reconstructive shoulder surgery from DR. FRANK JOBE, an orthopedic surgeon who invented the "TOMMY JOHN" (pitcher for LOS ANGELES DODGERS) surgery that baseball players were starting to embrace to lengthen their career.

ROSCOE decided to try my aqua therapy for rehab and strengthening his surgically repaired shoulder. Remember he had the biggest and fastest serve in the history of the game. 153 mph! Wooden racquet!

So on our first day in the pool at MISSION HILLS COUNTRY CLUB, RANCHO MIRAGE, CALIFORNIA, ROSCOE jumped into the water, and I almost had to save him from drowning. As he attempted to swim freestyle, he slowly sank like a submarine going into dive mode.

I had compassion since he was just coming off shoulder reconstructive surgery and could not rotate the shoulder or had the strength to pull water to swim.

This form of rehabilitation was unheard of at the time. ROSCOE was well known in tennis and wanted to continue playing and doing serve exhibitions in the game.

DR. FRANK JOBE inquired about his program, new trainer, and his techniques. Over the years, various teams, doctors, and schools would visit to make sure their stars were in good hands.

DR. FRANK JOBE came out to MISSION HILLS to meet and observe what I was doing. I was a nobody working with his tennis star. After watching what I was doing, DR. FRANK JOBE embraced my program. I continued to work in various capacities with DR. FRANK JOBE until a few years before his passing in 2014.

ROSCOE and I were like two adopted brothers who finally met after being separated all the years. We had a similarity to each other. We were personable, quick-witted, knowledgeable, STANFORD connection, and much more. Numerous times, people would mistake me for ROSCOE TANNER because I was in great shape and looked like a professional tennis player.

So as our friendship grew. ROSCOE served came back stronger, faster, and he lost about 10–15 lbs., and was able to hang in rallies.

When opponents faced "SCOE," they would have to handle his serve and start a rally because "SCOE" could only hit about half a dozen balls in a rally, and the point would be over.

ROSCOE had built a new base and foundation for his game to withstand a rally of more than ten shots. We religiously got up 6:00–8:00 a.m. to work on conditioning and tennis stroke production. Returning to serve was always challenging!

We traveled throughout the country conducting tennis clinics and exhibitions, and ROSCOE displayed the power of his service motion, and the new racquets kept him in the game.

I experienced what most people will NEVER get the opportunity to have, to attempt returning one of the game's historic and biggest serves. Thousands of opportunities!

I remember in Arkansas when the state police escorted us to a club from the airport and used their radar guns to clock the speed of ROSCOE'S serve. Over time, I was able to read his serve and luckily got a frame to bunt back his serve, and sometimes, he could return with some pace. Numerous times, I got pegged with a little ice treatment later!

One of his greatest stories and television videos he showed me was as a TEAM tennis member.

His team was playing at the "FORUM" in INGLEWOOD, CALIFORNIA, and the home of the LOS ANGELES LAKERS.

The opponent's team had BRAD GILBERT as their top player.

The format of team tennis was singles (men or women), doubles (men and women), and finally mixed doubles (man and women playing together).

ROSCOE had just finished having surgery on his serving shoulder (lefty) and was in a recovery period (before we got together).

ROSCOE was watching the final match of the night, mixed doubles. His opponent's mixed doubles team included BRAD GILBERT who was taking shots at ROSCOE women player on his team. Literally trying to tag her, which is a good shot, BRAD was consistently trying to hit her.

In team tennis, you can substitute a player at any time.

ROSCOE was fuming on the sidelines with BRAD'S taking cheap shots at his female teammate!

ROSCOE substituted himself into the match.

He came into the match to deliver serve. Even though he was still recovering from surgery (DR. FRANK JOBE), he was going to teach BRAD GILBERT a lesson!

BRAD GILBERT stood in position to return ROSCOE'S serve.

You must remember he had not hit a serve for months.

ROSCOE was so pissed off with GILBERT taking cheap shots at his female teammate.

So he prepared to serve. He was going to serve BRAD the biggest serve in his career no matter how much his arm might hurt or delay his recovery.

Low ball toss, he connected his lefty serve in the sweet spot of his racquet, and the ball hit the middle of service court to BRAD's forehand. The ball skidded and hit into BRAD jewels!

This moment is recorded for television!

The ball speed and power of the service ball landed and lifted BRAD two-to-three inches off the ground, and BRAD landed on his back with the ball still stuck between his legs in the nut sack! BRAD was knocked out!

ROSCOE, in commentary, as we watched the replay video at his home, said, "It was the hardest and best serve of his career, at least 160 mph." He said his arm needed another few weeks to recover!

This moment was one of his happiest moments in tennis!

Another time ROSCOE and I were ten-to-fifteen handicappers in golf. We were in KAUAI LAGOONS, KAUAI, HAWAII.

We had a contract to conduct tennis and training clinics at the resort. We weren't paid for our numerous visits but did receive first-class roundtrip air transportation, a $500.00 stipend each day for us, (I will tell you it sounds great, but you can never spend that much), unlimited golf, and limousine transportation.

ROSCOE and I were featured on the resort television daily on a loop, a flyer into every room with bedside chocolate, and were subjected to be available at any time a guest had a tennis question or needed a spontaneous pool instruction workout.

MARK AGUIRE of WORLD CHAMPION DETROIT PISTONS asked for a few spontaneous aqua/pool workouts.

Our tennis clinic day for resort guests was canceled with a small hurricane coming through the island. We saw an opportunity and talked to the golf professional to let us go out and play.

We were challenged by the wind coming in every direction along with the rain. I think they had sixteen inches of rain from this storm! We played about forty glorious holes and lost very few balls. It was so much fun!

I became the DIRECTOR OF SPORT and TRAINING at RUPERT MURDOCH'S (Murdoch-owned DOLE PINEAPPLE, a few other major companies, and 90 percent of ISLAND of LANAI, which was sold to LARRY ELLISON) new residential community in LAKE SHERWOOD, and SHERWOOD COUNTRY CLUB. I was under the direction of ROSCOE TANNER, director of tennis and fitness spa.

I assisted and designed the tennis center at SHERWOOD COUNTRY CLUB. ROSCOE wanted a larger northern window so we could see RUPERT MURDOCH when SHERWOOD COUNTRY CLUB owner, president, and CEO would leave his ranch and approach the property.

Good design!

Please read in the golf section about SHERWOOD COUNTRY CLUB and THE GREG NORMAN SHARK SHOOTOUT, and our days with GREG NORMAN and THE SHARK SHOOTOUT with RUPERT MURDOCH.

I was one of RUPERT MURDOCH'S favorite employees. He respected that I owned a business and would commute to THOUSAND OAKS and give 100%+! Personable and accountable, and would assist when we had to adjust on the fly. RUPERT MURDOCH'S employee's favorite saying is, "He would chew you a new asshole if you didn't show your mettle."

I had a great time.

Roscoe burned to many bridges. ROSCOE was GREAT with everyone. Sometimes overextending his greatness. He's a good guy and has a good heart when one on one!

DERRICK ROSTAGNO

A southern CALIFORNIA player who was the son of parents who were musicians and teachers.

A handsome guy who had success on the ATP Tour.

We met when I coached and traveled with various professional ATP and WTA players.

We shared the common connection of the ocean waves. He loved to surf whenever he had the opportunity.

He had two surf vans parked on the EAST and WEST coasts. They were always packed and ready to go! When he got a break on the tour, he would jump at the chance to ride a few waves if there was a swell.

He would visit my business and park the VW Surf Van on a slight hill. Occasionally, the van would not kick over, and being on a hill, he would release the brake and jump-start the van at 20 mph. A few times, my customers and I would assist in pushing and running to get the van enough speed to jump-start. One time, we pushed the van about half a mile until DERRICK got it started.

We caught up with each other again at the WIMBLEDON players' lounge upstairs. The player I was working with was also from SOUTHERN CALIFORNIA, and he was a friend.

My guy was a prankster. One of his favorite things to catch a person off guard was a fake sneeze. He would dip his fingers in his water glass without you noticing, and unexpectedly do a fake sneeze with the water on his fingers at you. The person getting sneezed on had no clue that the fluid you were getting hit was just water.

Let me tell you that DERRICK didn't like the joke and he was not happy.

This tournament for DERRICK was the most memorable tournament for a young seventeen-year-old who went on to win and became the star! Six major titles, forty-nine tournament victories, twenty-five-plus million in prize money, and back-to-back WIMBLEDON titles.

DERRICK had a match point against BORIS BECKER in the first round and was moving forward in a great position to the net to hit the return from BORIS BECKER. DERRICK was in volley forehand position. BECKER'S shot hit the top of the net tape and bounced over DERRICK and dropped in for a winner. BECKER went on to beat DERRICK and steamrolled to the first of his back-to-back WIMBLEDON titles!

FEMALE PLAYERS' STORIES

BILLIE JEAN KING, ROSIE CASALS, MARTINA NAVRATILOVA, PAM SHRIVER, CHRIS EVERT, TRACY AUSTIN, CAMMI MACGREGOR, CINDY MACGREGOR, JENNIFER SANTROCK, BETSY NAGELSON MCCORMACK, STEFFI GRAF, ANN GROSSMAN, DESIREE KRAZJECK, COCO VANDEGWHEE, PATRICIA TIG, ALAXANDRIA STEVENSON, ARYNA SABALENKA, VANESSA WEBB, MARY PIERCE.

I grew up in PALO ALTO, STANFORD, CALIFORNIA. A tennis mecca for tennis enthusiasts. The home of STANFORD UNIVERSITY.

PALO ALTO/STANFORD had a sporting goods store called SPIRO'S at Town and Country Village shopping center. The store was directly across the street from STANFORD UNIVERSITY and my high school, PALO ALTO HIGH SCHOOL, built on land deeded by the founder of STANFORD UNIVERSITY, LELAND STANFORD.

My mother played tennis and competed in numerous CALIFORNIA STATE CHAMPIONSHIPS. Please look at the entry fees. Mom coached at two private girls' schools: CASTILLEJA and SACRED HEART Catholic schools. My mother gave lessons to SHIRLEY TEMPLE.

My parents had their first date on a tennis court!

Anyway, back to the story. Occasionally, SPIRO'S would have athletes appear for a "Greet and Meet" (that's what it is called in 2022) at the store.

The first time I met BILLIE JEAN KING was when she appeared at SPIRO'S in 1970 as the finalist at WIMBLEDON Women's CHAMPIONSHIPS with only about a crowd of twenty people showed up to meet her.

In another time that our paths crossed again was at the U.S. OPEN (before honoring tennis championship and naming it THE BILLIE JEAN TENNIS CENTER in FLUSHING MEADOWS).

My players had just won a historic doubles WIMBLEDON CHAMPIONSHIP 7–6 (5), 7–6 (5), 7–6 (5) and were ranked #1 in the world in doubles.

Our practice court area was surrounded by about fifty-to-hundred people watching various courts. BILLIE JEAN KING was on the court adjacent to our court working with a young junior.

I noticed my guys were feeling a little tired and just didn't have it to practice.

I pulled them up to the net and suggested, "Let's do something different?" I announced to the spectators, "Anyone who had tennis shoes on can come out with someone else and play KING OF THE COURT until you lost the point?" Soon, the crowd grew from a few to almost five hundred plus!

It was a GREAT DAY for tennis spectator enthusiasts.

Talk of the early tournament, a fabulous and memories for a life. The ONLY person who objected was BILLIE JEAN KING!

ROSIE CASALS was and still is a close and best friend of BILLIE JEAN KING.

They teamed up to win numerous tournaments and tennis majors.

I run into ROSIE CASALS since she is a local resident. ROSIE is always outgoing and friendly.

MARTINA NAVRATILOVA. I had the opportunity to participate in the MARTINA GETAWAY VACATIONS in the island of ANTIGUA. A tennis package to meet, play, and entertainment with MARTINA.

I was one of the tennis team that included PAM SHRIVER and a few others. TENNIS MAGAZINE SHOW nationally syndicated television show (before tennis channel) filmed daily; and included featuring me in numerous segments (Remember tennis training was relatively new).

We took over the ST. JAMES CLUB in ANTIGUA.

A beautiful resort on the ocean. The resort has a casino, yachts, sailing, tennis courts, great food, service, accommodations, and the beaches were pristine.

It was a rough time for MARTINA since she was breaking up her relationship with JUDY NELSON.

MARTINA came into my cafe, and I had to remind her of our weeks together. She was startled to see her pictures from ANTIGUA and the gracious "Thank You" she had sent me (I realize the words were probably written by an agent).

PAM SHRIVER is an interesting person, and a tennis player.

We had an interesting moment in guest's player questions. A guest asked both MARTINA and PAM if they thought "going at your opponent with your shot is a good play." And they said NO!

I intervened and disagreed with them!

JENNIFER SANTROCK, SMU, and I felt the sexiest and great looking female on the tour at the time. She was brilliant thinker on the court, had fun, and very personable.

JENNIFER was a person who taught me a lot of loyalty, commitment, and to be more professional.

JENNIFER teamed up with a young rookie named MARY PIERCE, fifteen in doubles. MARY had the thickest glasses I had ever seen. Her father sold everything and bought a motorhome and the whole family lived and traveled in the motorhome.

MARY PIERCE won the FRENCH OPEN and was able to provide a home for her family. MARY PIERCE was a tough player and competitor.

Anyway, back to MARTINA and PAM SHRIVER at ANTIGUA, ST. JAMES CLUB, and about doubles.

My guys were #1 in the world in doubles, and going at your opponent is a GREAT shot especially if they have great reactions at net! I shared that my player who is ranked #1 in the world in doubles doesn't like to be pegged or attempted to and he is a bit more tentative to get to the net.

Today's game. Some female players will play off the back!

CHRIS EVERT married GREG NORMAN, a major fault! I could never figure out that relationship benefits. I conducted a few clinics where her father was involved in FLORIDA with ROSCOE TANNER.

TRACY AUSTIN is someone who keeps showing up in broadcasts. Her brother JOHN AUSTIN and I worked together for years.

TRACY AUSTIN accomplished two U.S. OPEN WOMEN'S SINGLES CHAMPIONSHIPS in succession. She had a game and youth which was advantageous.

I gave up watching matches that she broadcasts on television because she basically says the same thing about every player.

Her insight to the game is not the same when she played. Only about experiences of winning championships young.

CAMMI and CYNTHIA McGREGOR, the sisters. I really enjoyed these two and thier parents.

I ran into CAMMI at a gym and introduced myself and said, "If you ever need a trainer, chef, mental coach, here is my number."

I found my number I had given her on the floor at the gym. CAMMI just crumbled it up and threw it away.

Her parents had their residence down the street from my parents at PGA WEST. They would get together at club functions, etc.

CAMMI and CYNTHIA played doubles together. CAMMI was an extrovert, and CYNTHIA was an introvert.

I was working with players and traveling the tours. They would always have their parents on tour with them.

I was at the NASQUE 100 in BOCA RATON, FLORIDA and CAMMI, CYNTHIA, and her mother approached me in the players dining lounge.

They asked me if I would be interested in traveling and coaching/training their daughters? Sure.

CAMMI was a fiery red-heat, and CYNTHIA was a blonde tall mellow player.

CAMMI played singles too. She had made it to quarterfinals of AUSTRALIA OPEN earlier in year. Her temper was her biggest obstacle to overcome.

CAMMI was playing the #9 player in singles, SANDRA CICHINNI, in TAMPA, FLORIDA. CAMMI WAS down 6–0, 5–0 and 30 love. SANDRA was two points from victory.

CAMMI just lost it when her return was called long and now faced match point on clay. CAMMI just went ballistic, loud profanity, throwing her racquet, and acting like a complete non-professional.

The tournament official who I knew well due to traveling on the tour came out onto the court. I started speaking out "Don't def her. Don't def her." (Meaning defaulting her, to lose)

CAMMI had a "foul" mouth worse than anyone I knew!

The tournament official gave her a brake and let her continue and she came back and won 0–6, 7–5, 7–5, and defeated the number ten player in the world.

Sadly, years later, CYNTHIA fell down a flight of stairs and died. CAMMI's father died a few months before. I cooked and comforted the CAMMI and her mom for a few weeks.

I trained BETSY NAGELSON MCCORMACK who married MARK MCCORMACK, founder of IMG.

We only had a few sessions at MISSION HILLS COUNTRY CLUB, RANCHO MIRAGE.

BETSY had a fabulous career and retired and enjoyed the IMG. BETSY was a commentator for tennis but it wasn't her calling.

BETSY lives in FLORIDA, a single mother, and who is wonderful and proactive with her daughter. BETSY is a dog lover as well!

I coached/trained/chaperoned a group of five twelve-year-old tennis players in the EUROPEAN JUNIOR DAVIS CUP CHAMPIONSHIPS. I did not tell BETSY about my involvement until I returned from EUROPE. Five countries and seven tournaments.

The hitting partner coach was twenty-four, and dating a fifteen-year-old. FIFTEEN YEARS OLD!

My client paid the two hundred fifty thousand price tag because his twelve-year-old competed. It was a total disaster! I shared that with BETSY when I returned.

BETSY was responsible for bringing MARIA SHARAPOVA under her wing and her confidant for years!

My GOAT of women's tennis is STEFFI GRAF AGASSI. The only women in professional tennis to win all four MAJORS and OLYMPIC GOLD in the same calendar year.

For one year at the U.S. OPEN, the players I was working with were playing a night match. The player's lounge waiting area was semi-dark, low lighting and I was waiting for my guys. STEFFI GRAF was the only person besides myself in the room. STEFFI was personable and I hate to say it, "sweet as can be," then she finally was called to her evening match in a full packed stadium.

I am always questioning that the bandwagon only talks about SERENA and never acknowledging the GOAT, STEFFI GRAF.

ARYNA SABALENKA. My former player (DMITRY TUSUNOV, read about him in tennis chapter) coached an upcoming and eventual top ten WTA in the world.

SABALENKA'S coach chatted when she was playing in CANADA.

After watching her match on television, I shared with DMITRY that ARYNA could be top ten women player in the world.

For the next year, I would text DMITRY and consult and gave him some advice for her future tennis development.

I had the opportunity to meet ARYNA SABALENKA, but decided I enjoyed being a ghost trainer advisor.

ARYNA SABALENKA was playing ANGELIQUE KERBER at BNP INDIAN WELLS, a night match on center and it was televised. And an interesting moment when DMITRY was called down to the court on a changeover (some coaching is allowed at tournaments) during the changeover television showed nothing was said between the two but DMITRY did text me right after this coaching changeover.

DMITRY is like a son to me and he has a better side to him off the court. (Read about DMITRY further in this chapter.)

DESIREE KRAZJECK, a desert resident. I started working with her at seven years of age at MISSION HILLS COUNTRY CLUB, RANCHO MIRAGE.

We continued working as she grew up.

Her father, TEDDY, called DESIREE "BABY BULLIT." I really liked her father, he was different, but fun!

DESIREE even worked in my business for a few years.

Ask her about her eighteenth birthday celebration?

She won the FRENCH OPEN, WIMBLEDON, AND THE U.S. OPEN in MIXED DOUBLES in 2021!

A GREAT accomplishment! You also need a good doubles partner.

A few years ago, the tours changed the format best of three, and if you split sets, you go to a ten-point tiebreaker to ten. Must win by two points.

I'm sorry but when the athletes I worked with who captured MIXED DOUBLES titles, they had TOP competition. Top #20 players in singles but money has changed everything. The demand of singles is too tough on the body, and players are saving themselves in the majors.

ALEXANDRIA STEVENSON. I met ALEXANDRIA STEVENSON when her mother SAMANTHA STEVENSON came to KAUAI, HAWAII, for vacation and attended ROSCOE TANNER and myself tennis clinics where they were staying.

ALEXANDRIA was a twelve-year-old who was embracing the game under her mother's supervision and guidance. Her mother knew ALEXANDRIA had the goods to be a potential professional tennis player.

SAMANTHA was a leader in reporting and a terrific writer who broke the "locker room" barrier for female reporters. She was the first reporter in the men's locker rooms. She became a nationwide known reporter interviewing PRESIDENT JIMMY CARTER for PLAYBOY magazine.

ALEXANDRIA had an "up and down career." Her best result was a quarterfinal showing at WIMBLEDON. She can be seen and heard in television broadcasts.

AMY FRAZIER. I had the good fortune to work with this sweet, loyal, and world-class tennis player. AMY was a pupil of JOHN AUSTIN in LA QUINTA, CALIFORNIA.

For ten years, AMY FRAZIER was ranked in the top twenty WTA players in the world. AMY'S game consisted of heavy penetrating precision groundstrokes from corner to corner. AMY always gave 100+%!

I remember when she played the marque U.S. OPEN daytime match. JOHN McENROE called the match. MAC made a comment to the viewers "Not to adjust your television set because AMY is the palest, sun skin protection on the tour." AMY always used a few bottles of sun screen to avoid skin cancer.

We abruptly stopped working together when coach JOHN AUSTIN was fired earlier in the day from LA QUINTA COUNTRY CLUB for organizing the members to revolt removing the BEST grass courts in the desert to build more condos!

When AMY and I found out, we ended our training at the club!

AMY's mom like some tennis parents was always present!

COCO VANDEGWHEE. I also worked with her during her developing tennis career. Lots of coaches helped her, and she also spent a great deal of time in the desert.

I worked with her Uncle BRUK VANDEGWHEE, a professional volleyball player. We worked in VAIL, COLORADO, and LA QUINTA, CALIFORNIA.

COCO was having mixed results and would sometimes just implode on the court. She was gifted with GREAT DNA from her family.

COCO and her HALL OF FAME GRANDPA, the late DR. ERNIE VANDEGWHEE, the first sport's doctor who played for the NEWS YORK KNICKS. He was the first player in the NBA to room with a player of color. The JACKIE ROBINSON of NBA.

One of the most amusing scenarios happened at the U.S. OPEN when she was eighteen.

Her first match at the U.S. OPEN was against the #2 player in the world, and seeded second at the OPEN, and on national television as the introduction to a young AMERICAN star.

Earlier in the day, COCO signed her first major contract with NIKE. They interviewed her before she came onto the court, she was a "GIDDY" eighteen-year-old in a candy store. COCO was so excited to share on national television audience that she just had signed her first major contract endorsement!

Anyway Coco got drilled 6-2, 6-0, and even stumbled across the court with her new clothing digs. Her stumble was not graceful!

COCO being eighteen was still eligible to compete in the juniors since she lost early.

GUESS WHAT? COCO WON the U.S. JUNIOR GIRL'S CHAMPIONSHIP!

ANN GROSSMAN. She was tough and tenacious, she NEVER was NOT ready for an epic battle!

ANN always gave 100%+!

I wish more of the players I worked with, male and female, could embrace how she competed on the court, to destroy the opposition!

I spent some time with her whenever she came to the desert.

A USA OLYMPIC CHAMPION husband and a mother to two athletic sons! One of my favorites.

VANESSA WEBB was an NCAA CHAMPION at DUKE, UNIVERSITY, and an ALL ACADEMIC ALL-AMERICAN.

She was tall, 5'11, serve and volley lefty.

VANESSA came out to CALIFORNIA during her winter break from school at DUKE and resided in my home with my wife at the time. My wife and I had some challenging moments with deciding about raising a family.

This was VANESSA'S junior year. She had a busy schedule: academics, tennis, boyfriend, and attending one of the topo schools in the country.

So we synergized our thoughts and developed a program and schedule to be followed daily and sure enough, VANESSA stuck to the program and WON the NCAA SINGLES CHAMPIONSHIPS title and was honored to be the FIRST TEAM NCAA ACADEMIC ALL-AMERICAN.

At the BNP, she started to get into a car at BNP and to her surprise, it was me! I was surprised, ditto, I was not able to give her a ride since I was already assigned to go to the airport. Couldn't change my ride.

PATRICIA TIG. A new mother who got stuck in the desert due to COVID.

I was sitting on my deck and could hear that sweet sound of tennis ball being hit in the center of the strings. That is a different sound as a professional.

I ventured over to the court that sound was coming from. Inquired who they were, introduced myself, and we decided to spend a few lessons together.

If PATRICIA challenged her game, she could have had potential. Her focus was on being a mother, and her daughter #1.

Her boyfriend decided not to pay me. Four sessions, and I had to pay for all my own expenses, travel to out-of-town courts. Her boyfriend coach was a frustrated former top 200 tour player who thought he was the second coming of top coaches. Another lesson learned!

DICK GOULD

The winningest coach in NCAA history!
Seventeen!
He amassed seventeen NCAA titles!
I remember sitting with "COACH JOHN WOODN" and shared with him that I knew of a NCAA coach who won more NCAA titles than you and coached in the PAC 8–PAC 12!"
COACH JOHN WOODEN smiled and acknowledged COACH DICK GOULD'S accomplishments!
I shared with COACH WOODEN that COACH GOULD is a humble, motivating, stabilizing, and NOT a one-hit wonder championship like so many coaches!

All of COACH GOULD players, and former players, speak so highly of him and quietly "thank him" for his contributions in shaping the players future lives and their success.

COACH GOULD developed a HALL OF FAME team of players throughout the years. From ROSCOE TANNER, SANDY AND GENE MAYER (twins), JOHN AND PATRICK McENROE (brothers), SCOTT HUMPHRIES, JARED PALMER, DAVID WHEATON, JIM GRABB, JOHNATHAN STRAK, ALEX O'BRIEN, BOB AND MIKE BRYAN (twins), PAUL GOLDSTEIN, JIM THOMAS, TIM MAYOTTE, SCOTT DAVIS, JEFF TARANGO, please read STANFORD, NCAA player stories.

That's a "WHO'S WHO" of college players who also had historic professional careers.

My mother was a very good tennis player, a nationally ranked junior in the 1930s, later taught in the 1950s, and coached locally at two private girl schools in PALO ALTO and MENLO ATHERTON. Mom even gave local SHIRLEY TEMPLE tennis lessons (please refer to the numerous stories in other chapters) and her tennis connections is how she met COACH GOULD.

COACH GOULD met with future college players that I was traveling and coaching on a summer tournament tour trip. COACH took time out of his busy schedule to meet with us and gave everyone a tour of the tennis facility. Most importantly, giving guidance on their college future.

The new tennis complex and adjacent aquatic center is now where the STANFORD LACROSSE field used to be where I played for the STANFORD LACROSSE CLUB before the UNIVERSITY recognized the team and offered UNIVERSITY SCHOLARSHIPS!

COACH GOULD had a fixation of a classic MERCEDES that both my mother and I owned the same make and model.

COACH GOULD and his lifelong teammate ANN, wife, are now dedicating their life in helping in the area of "concussion and its consequences," their foundation.

PETE SAMPRAS

I first met PETE as a sixteen-year-old junior at MISSION HILLS COUNTRY CLUB, RANCHO MIRAGE.

Throughout the years, I would run across PETE since he lived in the same community where a few of my players resided. Specifically, the #! doubles player in the world. RANCHO PALOS VERDES resident, JIM PUGH.

PETE would be our "go-to" guy for a hitting partner and to play practice matches. We would meet at SOUTHEND TENNIS COMPLEX.

PETE was competitive and didn't like losing. PETE would occasionally call a shot out when the shot was in during our practice matches. That is something ALL juniors learn, and it's called HOOKING! PETE, additionally, would make up some lame excuse to stop playing when he started to lose and take advantage in our practice matches.

So finally, I told PETE that we were going to "finish what we started," and I was going to be the "CHAIR UMPIRE" and make the calls in our practice matches. Numerous times, I would force PETE to finish our practice matches. I felt this helped PETE and JIM win numerous CHAMPIONSHIPS in their career.

It was interesting result. Yes, PETE would dominate in the beginning. JIM would prevail as the practice match continued. JIM was the real big first guy on tour. 6'5" with great serve and volleys!

So it was ironic that a few weeks later, PETE and JIM would be playing each other in CINCINNATI at KING'S ISLAND. We also stayed in the players' hotel, and our rooms were adjacent.

We could hear PETE and his coach in animated conversations since we only had a door separating our suites. They broke the suite into two rooms due to lack of rooms to accommodate players.

PETE and JIM would meet in the quarterfinals. JIM and PETE played to a third set tiebreaker. JIM jumped out to a 5–2 lead. PETE hit a sitter that was in JIM'S 6"5" wheelhouse at the net especially the #1 doubles player in the world. A shot he could hit with his eyes closed, then JIM would have a handful of match points. JIM choked and totally whiffed the volley. PETE went on to WIN! That match changed his career.

PETE and I ran into each other again at the players hotel for WIMBLEDON, SAINT JAMES. (I was working with JIM PUGH AND JARED PALMER.)

We spoke for over an hour in the lobby. A wide range of topics especially the historic importance of WIMBLEDON.

A few months later, PETE would win the U.S. OPEN. The first of his fourteen GRAND SLAM titles.

The following week was a charity fund event in THOUSAND OAKS called the MUSIC and TENNIS FESTIVAL. The event raised money for providing music equipment for youth. The event included pro-am tennis and golf tournaments at SHERWOOD COUNTRY CLUB. ROSCOE and I were employed there.

At the opening tennis event, PETE was making his first news conference in SOUTHERN CALIFORNIA, his turf, after his dramatic U.S. OPEN win. The room was packed with media in an informal setting.

I arrived late and entered the room. PETE saw me out of the corner of his eye. PETE announced, "One more question?" Then PETE abruptly asked, "To clear the room?" And ended all questioning. PETE asked me to hang on. And in a few minutes, it was just PETE and I in the room.

PETE said to me, "CINCINNATI? And our chat in LONDON?" That win gave me the confidence to realize I can compete and WIN!

PETE would become a major champion fourteen times! PETE shares one of the GREATEST WIMBLEDON CHAMPIONS of all time! PETE could NEVER be considered the GOAT because he NEVER won at ROLAND GARROS FRENCH OPEN. The same can be said about ROGER FEDERER. Yes, he won the FRENCH OPEN but without facing the GREATEST clay-court player of all time, RAFA NADAL!

PETE was very shy and introverted!

It was interesting that I ran into PETE at BIGHORN COUNTRY CLUB where he had become a homeowner to basically play golf! I had to remind him who I was. I thought that was normal for an unappreciative tennis player when they become famous in their eyes. He was not nice!

PETE married an actress and has a family and is living life out of the spotlight and the dream, he loves golf!

MISSION HILLS COUNTRY CLUB

The DIRECTOR of TENNIS was a former ATP professional, coach at SOUTHERN METHODIST UNIVERSITY, DALLAS, TEXAS, the late DENNIS RALSTON.

DENNIS RALSTON moved on from MISSION HILLS. The next in line was his assistant TOMMY TUCKER, a former bartender from NORTHERN CALIFORNIA.

TOMMY was a personable and engaging man who was well-liked by members, guests, and professional athletes. MISSION HILLS had a "WHO'S WHO" of celebrity athletes. Additionally, the club was well known throughout the tennis community.

TOMMY inquired about me when I started working with ROSCOE TANNER. TOMMY asked ROSCOE about his recent shoulder surgery and rehab and informed him if was working with me. "WHO IS THIS GUY?"

Our local newspaper, *The Desert Sun*, and valley magazine, *Palm Springs Life* had just written about me. A nobody, who started to become A somebody, who was contributing to people's success.

MISSION HILLS throughout the years had TANNER, CHANG, SAMPRAS, EVERT, COURIER, and so many players, it is hard to list them all. GOLFERS: ALCOTT, COPLES, and the DINAH SHORE LPGA MAJOR baseball: BRETT. LYNN.

TOMMY provided me with many opportunities. One of the most challenging was teaching TOMMY and his wife BETTY to become better swimmers. In a short period, they were ready to compete in mini triathlons if they wanted to! They were real troopers.

JUNIORS and JR. DAVIS CUP

I have been fortunate to assist numerous top talented junior tennis players.

As young as seven years of youth to teenagers, and then becoming young adults.

One of the youngsters went on to winning numerous WTA tournaments, winning MIXED DOUBLES MAJORS. ROLAND GARROS, FRENCH OPEN, THE CHAMPIONSHIPS at WIMBLEDON, and U.S. OPEN. (DESIREE KRAZJECK read her story in the women's section).

An additional few other juniors went on to winning college scholarships and winning NCAA CHAMPIONSHIPS (FIVE). Some players even went on to playing in the professional ranks and winning majors.

Over one hundred college scholarships and adding to the success of numerous programs.

I have conducted tennis camps, boarding summer camps, and traveled the globe monitoring the future development of players.

It was always a challenge because every parent thinks their daughter/son is the next major champion.

JIM PUGH

The first "BIG 6'5" tennis player! His nickname was "PREMANIS" because of his seven-foot wingspan.

JIM as a twelve-year-old was the number #1 twelve-year-old player in the world in his age group. He was a right-handed player at twelve but then he broke his right arm. So he did what most twelve-year-old boys do: switch to his left arm and become a lefty. As a fourteen-year-old, he soon became the #1 fourteen-year-old in the world playing left-handed. WOH!

When I first started to work with him, I arrived at his parents' and his home in RANCHO PALOS VERDES.

I waited for JIM to arrive home from his singles victory at HALL of FAME, NEWPORT, RHODE ISLAND. Everyone who enjoys tennis should put the TENNIS HALL of FAME on your visit list.

JIM SR., "BIG JIM" was 6'5" plus, fifty-year-old, 260 lbs., who played basketball at USC in the '50s. Our conversation included my love for basketball as well.

So while we waited for JIM JR., to arrive home, JIM SR., asked me if I wanted to play hoops and one on one with the basket on the tennis court side.

The game was competitive! We played to twenty-one and you had to win by two. The game lasted over two hours. Yes, two hours!

"BIG JIM" fouled me numerous times and bounced me into a fence surrounding the side court. I won but was exhausted guarding a 6'5" 260 lb. man. He didn't know that I was a very good athlete. I loved hoop, I played rugby, lacrosse, football, etc., so playing against a bigger guy was NEVER a problem. I played against 6'8"–7' ft. players in basketball.

After the game, he shook my hand and said, "I look forward to you working with my son!"

JIM was #1 in the world in doubles with USC RICK LEACH for a number of years. They were undefeated in DAVIS CUP (6–0), and won JIM won EIGHT GRAND SLAM TITLES.

MICHAEL CHANG

He came to MISSION HILLS COUNTRY CLUB to work with JOSE HIGUERAS. Additionally, a young PETE SAMPRAS joined him as well.

Within a short period of time, MICHAEL CHANG won the FRENCH OPEN at ROLAND GARROS.

MICHAEL traveled with his family, JOE (father), BETTY (mom), and CARL (brother).

At the time, USTA was subsidizing his tennis. USTA allocated monies for coaching and training.

After CHANG won the FRENCH OPEN, he signed close to five million dollars of new endorsements, contracts, and prize money.

So MICHAEL and the family told JOSE that the USTA will pay his weekly salary. His weekly salary was one thousand dollars!

KARMA works in mysterious ways. I told MICHAEL'S father at a tournament that he is going to have some hip issues if he continued his training route that he was taking. Sure enough, it happened.

I remember telling a confident friend of MARIA SHARAPOVA that she was going to have some shoulder issues early in her career.

VIJAY ARMITRAJ

The first player from INDIA to make it on the ATP TOUR and the first tennis player from INDIA to become an INTERNATIONAL movie star! The JAMES BOND franchise! He also produced numerous movies!

At one of the first SENIOR TENNIS CHAMPIONS events that ROSCOE TANNER put on in MONTECITO, CALIFORNIA, VIJAY ARMITRAJ was in the field.

VIJAY assumed I was a world-class tennis player and could warm him up before his first-round match. ROSCOE was asked by VIJAY, "If I could warm him up?" and ROSCOE said, "SURE!"

I was assisting in setting up areas for the day. I was dressed in tennis attire and ROSCOE came over to me and said, "VIJAY needs you to warm him up for his match." I said, "I'm a 4.5 player, you hit with him?" ROSCOE said NO!

After VIJAY won his match, VIJAY said to ROSCOE, "Your man warmed me up, I had more running in the warm-up than in the match!"

ROSCOE in front of me replied, "Look, you dominated the match and won comfortably, my guy, RANDY, did the job, and you can't argue that!" VIJAY is an ICONIC star in INDIA.

USTA

Just read my thoughts about USTA tennis and lack of!

It has gotten worst, and they, USTA, just throw away money without producing results. Remember the WILLIAMS sisters did it all on their own under RICHARD WILLIAMS.

They released "KING RICHARD" where WILL SMITH won the OSCAR portraying RICHARD WILLIAMS. Do you know that RICHARD WILLIAMS WAS NOT CONSULTED NOR CONTRIBUTED to the movie!

STAN SMITH

I spent an afternoon sitting next to STAN SMITH at WIMBLEDON during my player playing singles.

Our conversation was about the unique training methods/chef who was unheard of at the time. I was having success across the board!

He conversed with the new development of my work to the head of USTA development. PAUL ROETERT. I had been working with JOSE HIGUERAS for years.

PAUL ROETERT was entertaining. I was assigned a code name like a secret agent whenever I contacted him before cell phones.

STAN SMITH is from the old school.

AUSTRALIAN OPEN, FRENCH OPEN, WIMBLEDON, U.S. OPEN

Of the four GRAND SLAM tournaments throughout the world, the BEST tournament is the AUSTRALIAN OPEN.

From transportation, organization, food and beverage, and overall treatment of players, family, coaches, and guests.

WIMBLEDON is so historic and recognized as the "GRAND DADDY" of them all—has the best transportation of any tournament.

All the staff goes beyond the call of duty to assist in you getting to the tournament in a small village town.

FRENCH OPEN, ROLAND GARROS is the most cultural and sightseeing of the four SLAMS. The FRENCH TENNIS FEDERATION goes beyond the normal tournament stuff. PARIS is not cheap!

U.S. OPEN is the worst in my view! The fans are the loudest and most vocal!

DMITRY TURSUNOV

From "RUSSIA to CALIFORNIA," an adopted CALIFORNIAN! Dmitry left the SOVIET UNION at the age of twelve and landed in SACRAMENTO, GRANITE BAY, CALIFORNIA.

I first ran into DMITRY when he was seventeen years old playing in a challenger tennis tournament in APTOS, CALIFORNIA. We were occupying the same gym space and little did we know our paths would cross again.

I got a call from coach JOSE HIGUERAS asking me if I would be interested in working with a raw undisciplined talent possible top ten tennis player.

He wasn't excited to meet the guy who would spend three-to-five hours a day, four to six a week breaking his butt to take him to the next level. He had a productive year and broke into the top 100 in the ATP tennis rankings. As the next off-season approached, once again he came to the desert to work.

Our day would start with breakfast yoga at "café," then they would work with JOSE from 8:30 a.m. At 11:00 a.m., we then come in for lunch, then return to the court from 1:00 p.m. to 2:30 p.m., and then work with me from 4:00 p.m. to 6 p.m. We did this five to six days a week!

DMITRY and another player, VEHE (who later became SAM QUERREY'S coach), would volunteer and come in and work at my "CAFE." I usually always had players I worked with pull a shift at "café." This business also allowed me to experience their personalities, how they apply it in sport, organizational skills, challenges, and other characteristics that they respectively approach their game and employment.

I faced adversity when my father passed while he was here training with me. I kept my father's health issues to myself to NOT interfere with my commitment to my job. My father passed early in the day. My father embraced the tenacity of this young athlete, DMITRY, and out of respect for my father's coaching background, I didn't miss a beat and fulfilled my working obligation. With a heavy heart, I finally privately shared with DMITRY my father's passing earlier in the day. A few days before DMITRY and my DECEMBER birthdays.

DMITRY and VEHE knew I was hurting and they came and worked every free moment they had to assist me in getting through the days. DMITRY also came and helped at my father's closed memorial with family members.

Yes, he won seven ATP tournament titles and won a historic DAVIS CUP for RUSSIA against ANDY RODDICK and the USA in MOSCOW. He won and collectively made bucks in earnings in his career.

Presently, he has coached WTA players to top ten rankings in the world (I consulted, text, with one gal) and continues to be a "RARE" guy! I would take a bullet for my young adopted son. "GODSPEED, MY BUD."

BNP VOLUNTEERING TRANSPORTATION

Niculeseu (Romania), Rybakina (Russia), Bouskova (Czech), Kasatkina (Russia), Krejcikova (Czech), Bencic (Swiss), Juvan (Slov), Fernandez (Canada), McNally (USA), Kerber (Germany), Kuntuh (Croatia), Haddad Maia (Brazil), Martic (Serbian), Kudermetova (Russia), Wozanacki (Denmark), Stubbs (Aussie), Elekri (Norway), Cornet (French)., Zheng (ATP)

German, Australian, Serbian, Italian, Spain, Argentina, Brazil—the tennis federations.

HOLOGIC -New global sponsor of WTA Tour, March 4, 2022, a medical technology company. I provided chamber of commerce moments about INDIAN WELLS and PALM DESERT.

AGENTS I drove and some of the clients they represented: WME/IMG—Jabeur, Hart, Fernandez, Osaka, and many more!

I was sitting at an outside coffee cafe in late September with a friend when RAY MOORE, CEO and founder of the BNP tournament cruised by.

My friend sitting with me had volunteered at the BNP in transportation for years.

The BNP was being played in October at a time when seasonal residents normally are not here. Due to COVID-19, the Canadian seasonal residents were not here as well due to the closing of the border. Additionally, the local golf courses are reseeding, temperatures are in mid-105 degrees, and this is NOT a time to visit the desert.

BNP having the tournament at this time was trying to recoup financial losses of the tournament not being played in March on the usual schedule. One of the reasons scheduling currently is that the success of "OLD-CHELLA" (Music festival with THE WHO, NEIL YOUNG, BOB DYLAN, THE ROLLING STONES, PINK FLOYD), which is like "Night and Day" to an attending tennis tournament at this time of year. "OLD-CHELLA" was successful beyond the projected financial models.

So conversing with RAY MOORE, he shared they needed volunteers for the October tournament. I said to RAY, "You have to pay me?" My friend shared that "I am not here that time of year." I knew RAY MOORE throughout the years, training and swimming lessons with his ex-wife and his daughter.

So the regular scheduled tournament was approaching. I decided that I need to pay back to a game that gave me so much. This tournament has been "very good to me, and my businesses."

I had to buy a pair of blue pants for my transportation uniform to be complete. Fila hat, Fila shirt, and Fila warm-up jacket for the desert cool nights—all were provided by tourney.

Many volunteers work basically for tennis tickets, meals, and parking privileges. Many volunteers are starstruck on who they will be assigned in transportation.

I drove a player who earned over forty million in prize money and was married to a former NBA player. We were called to provide two suburbans to the airport and another driver to return the BMW that the tournament provided them, for the three of us.

The other two drivers were commenting on how "RICH" the party we were going to transport to the airport. The group included a nine-month-old baby girl.

The problem with all these volunteer drivers is they get starstruck with who they are transporting to from the destination. I could care less who is in my car! I get my guests safely and quickly to their destination.

After my commitment of driving thirteen to fourteen days/evenings, I looked forward to not driving. I thoroughly looked forward to spending time with my dogs!

If you have an opportunity to volunteer in your community or visit a community that may need assistance in an event to happen, do it! It's GREAT to get an insight of what your volunteer commitment can do for its success. You get firsthand experience to see what goes on behind the scenes.

I enjoyed surprising former players when they saw me behind my Covid mask. It was entertaining to mix with the new sponsor of WTA Tour (Hologic) who I personally introduced them to our area. Chair umpires invited me to dinner in their hotel parking lot with their traveling kitchen equipment (it brought back memories of what I did on the tour). An upper WTA official who was emotional with the recent loss of her mother in my transport (I got to her destination but we spoke for fifteen minutes where I hopefully comforted her and had compassion and empathy).

A FRENCH WTA player who has earned over nine million and really enjoyed her time during the tourney, dining, dancing, etc. "BREATH OF FRESH AIR." And a top seventy-ranked WTA player who travels with her father and was ecstatic about qualifying and getting into the main draw hotel. She was outgoing, bubbly, and couldn't stop laughing and smiling.

I ALWAYS asked my passenger(s) if they wanted to talk or not. On some airport runs, I would show them "EISENHOWER HOSPITAL," "BETTY FORD CENTER," "BARBARA SINATRA CHILDREN'S CENTER," "ARNOLD PALMER CANCER CENTER," all tennis sponsors, then "ANNENBERG ESTATE," "FRANK SINATRA'S" home then the home of the original BNP site (PILOT PEN, MISSION HILLS COUNTRY CLUB) all are part of the continued success of this tournament.

Only two of my transportation rides were not enjoyable. Two female young doctors who were starstruck and felt they knew everything. I shared with them it is hard to relate to conditions, injuries, and situations that may contribute to an inaccurate analysis of an athlete when they have NEVER participated in sports. It is very difficult to assess something if you have NEVER been a part of it. Then the other is a gentleman with his wife who in our entire ten-mile ride never got off the phone with attorneys making sure to protect a player and having prepared selective questions to the athlete to spin a narrative to an athlete who grossed millions the year before.

TENNIS players are cheap. I am justified to make that statement being on the ATP/WTA tour for years trying to save the buck. Most players will eat at the tournament site instead of having to go off-site. My "Cafe" was a player "Hotspot" for years until the BNP added twenty restaurants to keep players on-site with "NO" reason to spend money when everything was free.

Some stories of the most recent tournament in 2022. A WTA player who had five rooms, yes, five rooms called the bellman and his staff to help move their twenty-five-plus bags to transport. The bellman's crew was shorthanded and moved everything for transport. The player stiffed the bellman crew, YES stiffed them a big fat "0!"

Then the bellman shared a player who had food delivered to the hotel. Due to Covid, the bellman is NOT allowed to handle food, or deliver it to the guests. The player called for the head bellman and said, "I will give you a big tip if you deliver to my room." The bellman shared with me "Look at my BIG tip, $1 dollar." The bellman kept the ticket in his special clothing pocket to share with the staff "how big spenders tip." Then one of the top WTA players had a party of six at a local nationally-known restaurant chain that had a bill over one thousand dollars and stiffed the server and staff. Yes, stiffed 0! A big fat 0!

It was my "PAYBACK" like I said.

The tournament had a "thank you" dinner for all the volunteers. The dinner was well attended by almost seven-hundred folks! I was shocked that neither RAY MOORE, CEO, OR TOMMY HAAS were

"NO SHOWS" to "thank" the volunteers who make this tournament happen! I still find it hard to comprehend that the majority of the volunteers have NO clue who these two guys are.

The CHEF and staff did an outstanding job!

For the record, I NEVER used any of the tickets, meal vouchers, or parking pass during the entire duration of the tournament. A first for BNP!

BNP

This tournament grew from a small event venue in the desert, COACHELLA VALLEY, to become one of the world's top five tournaments. Most tennis recognizes the BNP to be the fifth major, one of the strongest field's participation from the ATP/WTA tours.

One of the historic tournaments with crowds of over four hundred thousand spectators.

The players look forward to coming to the desert due to all the player perks. Now with LARRY ELLISON, one of the wealthiest men in the world, makes it almost impossible not to attract the world's best players.

From golf, accommodations, transportation, food, and beverage, if you lose, you are still allowed a few more days, and the prize money is ridiculous.

The weather is a big plus!

Recently, the CEO, a former player, made some disparaging remarks about the WTA women's tour and faced the consequences. Basically, he still ran the tournament and still remains the "man in charge" today.

History will tell you it's a tough business to be in! The ONLY difference is the BNP has an owner who happens to be one of the wealthiest businessmen in the world! Money is not a deterrent to having deep pockets for a sport you embrace.

The CEO should be happy that he loves this game!

POLITICS

A subject that most individuals try to avoid is the subject that has contributed to ending friendships and employment, and even caused divorces.

The "golden rule" of social interaction is NOT to have political conversations.

The definition of "POLITICS" in the Webster Dictionary: "Politics is the activities, actions, of politics that are used to gain and hold power in a government or to influence a government. A person's opinions about the management of government."

The definition of "POLITICS" in the Urban Dictionary: "Derives from the root word "poly" meaning "many ticks" and "bloodsucking insects" and in this context means that the situation is about to get worse."

From the beginning. Presidents: Eisenhower, Kennedy, Reagan, Ford, Clinton, Trump. VPs: Ford, Quayle, Agnew. Senators: Boxer, Harkin, Alton, Feinstein. Cabinet: Kennedy, Harken, Monagen. Governors: Wilson, Schwarzenegger, Reagan, Agnew. Mayors: Moscone, Young, Jackson. Ambassadors: Young, Pope, Pope Paul VI, Kings. Generals: Dwight D. Eisenhower, General Westmoreland, Admiral Tom Lynch, General John Walker. Social Issues: Cuba, Vietnam, Civil Rights, Black Panthers, SLA. And numerous others. And most importantly being,

"AMERICAN, THE GREATEST COUNTRY IN THE WORLD"

"THE CIRCLE OF LIFE"

My introduction to "POLITICS" started with the former "PRESIDENT DWIGHT DAVID EISENHOWER" as a young child and continues to this day.

"CIRCLE OF LIFE," "EISENHOWER," saved my adult and quality of life even in 2022 and beyond.

The roaring blades of a helicopter and the charge of the wind from the blades. The former PRESIDENT was attending a NAVAL ACADEMY FOOTBALL game to watch the future HEISMAN TROPHY winner, ROGER "THE DODGER" STAUBACH. I was a short distance away from the former PRESIDENT, but his presence with security had a lasting impact on me. He lit a fire of curiosity with me. Endless questions to my parents about politics and "EISENHOWER" representing the AMERICAN people and what the office stood for one-hundred eighty million people in this country in 1960 (over three hundred million in 2021). Then later in life, I moved to Rancho Mirage in CALIFORNIA. I had volunteered at a hospital in SAN FRANCISCO (I enrolled in a graduate program that accepted me and part of the requirement for taking the class was to volunteer in a medical field position. I conducted maternity tours in a hospital) and explored and entertained the idea of being a volunteer at EISENHOWER HOSPITAL in RANCHO MIRAGE. I had a conflict with scheduling due to my new employment at the EISENHOWER HOSPITAL and I had numerous events that shaped my life. I was a sports trainer who was fortunate enough for athletes to attain or be considered for college academic/athletic scholarships. Most of the doctors were overwhelmed with their practices, building client base, research, additional studies, and most importantly families. I became a surrogate parent for the times that they did not have for their children. Most importantly, their lack of parenting and being involved with their children's extracurricular activities. My first doctor clients were two high school baseball players and brothers. Their father was the head ANESTHESIOLOGIST at EISENHOWER HOSPITAL. Both brothers played Division 1 baseball. And after graduating, it opened a very successful business that continues to be strong in 2022. After that, I started to mentor a young man occasionally whose father was a top specialist in MAXOFACIAL and DENTAL, PLASTIC SURGEON.

Then the DIRECTOR OF NEUROLOGY had two sons who played tennis. They were thirteen and fourteen years of age. They went on to become a successful attorney and the other a doctor. Then the HEAD OF EAR, NOSE, and THROAT had two sons as well who became a doctor and a concert promoter. The founder of the BETTY FORD CENTER had a son who was a baseball player who went into working with a major NEW YORK WALL STREET firm. The connections are that all the parents were all on the EISENHOWER HOSPITAL staff and working on campus later in life. Both of my parents died of cancer at eighty-seven at EISENHOWER HOSPITAL in 2015, May 23. I had a mountain bicycle accident in our local mountains and did not see a doctor until June 28. For a month, I walked around playing sports without knowing the severity of my injuries. My doctor friends mentioned above contacted a neuro-spinal surgeon who was on his first vacation in a few years to see if he would return for an emergency examination. I did not even know this doctor, he jumped on a plane, arrived at his office at 9:00 a.m., and looked at me, ran some tests, and by 10:00 a.m., I was in an intensive care and scheduled for surgery the next morning after the conclusion of MRI, X-RAYS, etc. I had been walking around, working in both businesses, with two compressed vertebrae, they were removed and replaced with a titanium plate, screws, bolts, and two broken wrists! My life was saved at EISENHOWER HOSPITAL, the "CIRCLE of LIFE." Additionally, on the EISENHOWER CAMPUS was the world-famous "BETTY FORD CENTER" which was founded by the former first lady of the UNITED STATES. BETTY FORD and JOHN SCHWARZOLOSE who was the director of the center for twenty-five years. I trained the director's son in baseball. BARBARA SINATRA had the CHILDREN'S CENTER and the LUCY CURCI CANCER center which both were fabulous and had outstanding facilities. Both my parents were patients at the LUCI CURCI CANCER CENTER. It is important to establish a relationship with your physicians and the hospital that you will frequent.

My mother was a devout ROMAN CATHOLIC and my father was IRISH CATHOLIC. My mother was a practicing CATHOLIC while my father just did what he had to do to appease my mother, and to know how to handle the questions with the right answers to keep mom's family happy. Our dinners were fish on Fridays. No swearing, etc. The excitement in our house was when the first presidential candidate was JOHN F. KENNEDY, the first ROMAN CATHOLIC to run for the highest office in the land. In the early sixties, my family resided in Annapolis, Maryland, due to my dad coaching the UNITED STATES NAVAL ACADEMY FOOTBALL TEAM. As a child, I was introduced to the possibility of war with the "BAY OF PIG'S MISSILE CRISIS" confrontation with NIKITA KRUCHEF. Our nanny and my mother went to the store to shop and load our basement with supplies to last a week to a month. Cooler heads prevailed, and JOHN F. KENNEDY stood his ground and prevented an all-out war. Lots of pundits said "GOD" and "JFK" saved our butts. JOHN F. KENNEDY became a SAINT and like hero, and his popularity soared. JFK would attend the ARMY-NAVY football game in PHILADELPHIA every year. JFK was a WORLD WAR II NAVY hero with the story of "PT-109." He was a NAVY man. JFK would sit on one side of the field for the first half of the ARMY-NAVY game and then would walk across the field to sit on the other team's stands. One year, he started on the NAVY side for the first half and then before the second half kickoff, he would be escorted by the MISSHIPMEN guard to mid-field and be given to the ARMY KNIGHTS precision. As he was walking to the ARMY side, he put both arms and hands behind his back and the stadium announcer would tell the crowd the PRESIDENT was going to sit on the ARMY side. And he made the "thumbs down" hand gesture behind his back which received a huge roar from the midshipmen and the NAVY fans. The following year, the NAVY FOOTBALL TEAM was one of the top four teams in the nation. The team had the "HEISMAN TROPHY" quarterback in ROGER "THE DODGER" STAUBACH. On an airport tarmac, PRESIDENT JOHN. F. KENNEDY made a surprise visit with the team and coaches. My father with a few other coaches was able to board the PRESIDENT'S plane and were given mementos. A few weeks later, I was playing at my elementary school and remember clearly the excitement of going to the ARMY-NAVY game that I shared with my teacher in the upcoming week. To this day, I remember her having a sad, frightened look on her face, and not really showing any reaction from my comments, hiding the news about THE PRESIDENT. A week earlier, my father was shaking hands and conversing about the war with PRESIDENT JOHN F. KENNEDY. And now the leader of the free world was assassinated. I wrote for our school paper and shared my visit a week later at the ARLINGTON CEMETERY and the "ETERNAL FLAME."

Later in life, I decided to work with "YOUNG DEMOCRATS for ROBERT KENNEDY" in CALIFORNIA. My older brother awakened me as ROBERT KENNEDY was giving his congratulations to CALIFORNIA voters for his victory in CALIFORNIA to be their candidate at the ROOSEVELT HOTEL when a gunman, SIHRAN SIHRAN, assassinated him. Earlier in the year, MARTIN LUTHER KING was assassinated. In a period of four months, we lost two polarizing figures for the future of our country. These events changed my perspective of change in our country. VIETNAM war was near its peak, and a few years later, I would become eligible for the draft. The DRAFT LOTTERY was instituted for young men to fight a war. Luckily, RICHARD NIXON declared that the lottery was unconstitutional. RONALD REAGAN had connections to the family as well. My father was at NOTRE DAME when "THE GIPPER" premiered. If you notice the program for the evening that RONALD REAGEN was misspelled, KEVIN SPACEY brought this to my attention then I was invited to "SAY NO TO DRUGS" at RIVIERA COUNTRY CLUB. My players were the number 1# doubles team in the world and WIMBLEDON reigning champions at the time. One of the selling points was JANE SEYMOUR was going to be one of the celebrities among the one hundred attendees. RONALD REAGEN had just had an accident where he was thrown off his horse at his ranch. He had a new wave haircut. At the end of the event, attendees were invited to have their picture taken with the former PRESIDENT and FIRST LADY. We stood in a line and waited for our opportunity to step in and have our picture taken. I noticed that no one even exchanged any dialogue or conversation with the PRESIDENT and FIRST LADY. My opportunity came. Out of NO disrespect, I said, "HEH, HOW YOU DOING TODAY?" They were startled at first because everyone just stood in line and waited for their opportunity to step in for their picture with them. The former FIRST LADY, NANCY replied, "THANK YOU FOR ATTENDING." And she noticed my tennis attire, so she followed up, "THE TENNIS HAS BEEN ENTERTAINING." I asked the former PRESIDENT HOW HE WAS FEELING? He replied, "I'M FEELING GREAT, THANKS." The press was going nuts because I was the ONLY one to create any dialogue with them.

I first ran into former PRESIDENT GERALD FORD at the "BOB HOPE DESERT CLASSIC" at INDIAN WELLS COUNTRY CLUB in California. Joining him were PRESIDENT BILL CLINTON, former PRESIDENT GERALD FORD, former PRESIDENT GEORGE BUSH, comedian and former host BOB HOPE, and former champion SCOTT HOCH. Obviously, it was a busy traffic day trying to get to our starting tee time at INDIAN WELLS COUNTRY CLUB. The traffic was backed up for miles in every direction to a club that ONLY had one entrance to handle the traffic. We were two miles away stuck in traffic, so the player I was caddying for, ROBIN FREEMAN, decided to take evasive action and maneuvered our vehicle on the sidewalk from Cook Street all the way to the club. ROBIN was the first-day leader shooting an opening-round sixty-three. Later in that tournament, our local golf writer, LARRY BOHANNON, wrote a story about caddying, owning a business, and a trainer who also taught yoga. About a month later, I got a call at my business around 6:00 a.m. The caller identified himself as a SECRET SERVICE agent for THE FIRST LADY. I said, "Right," and hung up. A few minutes later, I got a call again and the person said, "Don't hang up, I am calling on behalf of the FIRST LADY OF THE UNITED STATES, BETTY FORD" and told me to hang up and call this number. I called and was told that the FIRST LADY OF THE UNITED STATES would like to know if I was available to come to the FORD'S residence to teach a yoga class. MRS. FORD was a big yoga fan, and someone on her staff shared with her my article written and published in the paper, *The Desert Sun*. SECRET SERVICE requested for me if 6:00 a.m. would work for me. I said, "I own a business that requires me to shop daily, food preparation, a one-man show in the morning, and would not be able to." The agent said, "You're turning down the FIRST LADY of the UNITED STATES." I said, "I'm sorry but I am in business." Then my next rubbing elbows with PRESIDENT FORD was in VAIL, COLORADO, on July 4, where former PRESIDENT FORD was the grand marshal. We both lived in VAIL, COLORADO, during the summer (more in the golf chapter), then I caddied for my professional in the last year of GERALD FORD INVITATIONAL PRO-AM (will be covered in the music and golf chapter).

My friend opened and founded the BETTY FORD CENTER in RANCHO MIRAGE on the EISENHOWER HOSPITAL CAMPUS with the CEO and founder of BETTY FORD CENTER and the FORMER FIRST LADY. PRESIDENT BILL CLINTON. It was a brief encounter but he was gracious and very nice at BOB HOPE INVITATIONAL. During his presidency, I communicated by offering my services if he planned to play in any future events or at private courses in So-Cal. A winter destination for numerous PRESIDENTS was WALTER ANNEBERG'S estate in RANCHO MIRAGE, and to play the private golf course on his property that was only played with heads of state or dignitaries (more in golf chapter). It was always fun to get a letter from the WHITE HOUSE. PRESIDENT BARRACK OBAMA. He made numerous trips to the desert to play golf. One day, the SECRET SERVICE came into my establishment to scoop out the surroundings, check out the menu where I had some Hawaiian dishes, and ask some questions. The protocol with the PRESIDENT was to NEVER indulge information of itinerary of the PRESIDENT. I was excited and anxious of the possibility of a visit to my business. I even made a CD to give to him and the staff of GREAT MOTOWN HITS. He was a no-show. I crossed paths with the FIRST LADIES at BETTY FORD'S memorial.

MAYORS of ATLANTA ANDREW YOUNG and MAYNARD JACKSON. "BIG SERVE" ROSCOE TANNER and I were invited by the MAYOR to participate in "THE BOY'S and GIRL'S CLUB" of ATLANTA and "THE CHERRY BLOSSOM FESTIVAL" at the city park. We had just finished tennis events in HAWAII. We were the GUESTS of HONOR with other dignitaries for the FRIDAY night opening night and FUNDRAISING AUCTION, ETC. ROSCOE had too many cocktails so I took the PODIUM and spoke on both of our behalf. I was received with applause and concluded with applause. That evening, we were all taken to "RUTH CHRIS" for a dinner with thirty-plus people. I was introduced at the "FUNDRAISER" as "FUTURE DIRECTION OF SPORTS with TRAINING and NUTRITION." So ALL eyes were on me when I went to order in a "STEAK HOUSE." I ordered a plain salad, no dressing, tomatoes, etc., and a plain potato. I played the "GAME" to PERFECTION." I got immediate RESPECT. Only if everyone knew I was starving. When I got back to "THE RITZ CARLTON," I ordered room service and stuffed my face. The following day, we had an "OVER-THE-TOP" turn-out at the park for THE DOGWOOD FESTIVAL and THE BOY'S and GIRL'S CLUB. I worked my tail off running to various tennis courts to get everyone involved, even the kids who were having issues and emotions trying to hit tennis balls. It was a huge success. I even designed a training program for AMBASSADOR of THE UNITED NATIONS, ANDREW YOUNG. The following year, we were invited to return by new MAYOR MAYNARD JACKSON. We arrived early and were taken by limousine to a pancake breakfast house. ROSCOE and I were the only people of color to be in the restaurant by ALL the attention were for MAYOR MAYNARD JACKSON amongst his voters. The table was overwhelmed with well-wishers. We were scheduled to play golf and attend ATLANTA HAWK'S basketball game with DANNY GLOVER and MEL GIBSON. Our transportation NEVER showed up to take us to the game, so we got a cab. The limousine NEVER showed up to pick us up. We waited two hours. The following day, we were scheduled to play golf with the actors. I made the call to cancel since they showed complete disrespect to contact us and leaving us the night before. We had a FABULOUS day later doing an introduction clinic for one thousand ALTA members, the largest tennis membership of any tennis organization in the UNITED STATES with fifteen thousand plus members.

In my lifetime, I met and had conversations with a variety of GENERALS and ADMIRALS. GENERAL DWIGHT D. EISENHOWER and PRESIDENT of the UNITED STATES, GENERAL WESTMORELAND, GENERAL JOHN WALKER, ADMIRAL TOM LYNCH. (He played UNITED STATES NAVAL ACADEMY football, and was a team captain of the team with HEISMAN TROPHY winner ROGER STAUBACH.) GENERAL WESTMORELAND said to me, "There are three types of soldiers, ones who don't show up, show up, and soldiers . . ." And he said, "You would be one of my soldiers." 1968: April 4, and June 8. On April 4, MARTIN LUTHER KING was assassinated. My father was returning from a family vacation in Florida. He decided to take us to SELMA, ALABAMA, to experience MARTIN LUTHER KING'S MARCH the week before. The woman who worked for us missed a day of work at our home and attended "MARTIN LUTHER'S KING" speech in WASHINGTON, D.C. She said, "I HAVE BEEN TO THE MOUNTAIN TOP AND SEEN THE OTHER SIDE." Hearing those still resonates in my soul today. ROSEMARY was part of my family as a youth and was remarkable that my mother included and embraced this wonderful woman, where in the late thirties, my mother's brother was brutally murdered in a horrific crime. I think of "ROSEMARY" often when my family relocated back to CALIFORNIA from MARYLAND the day of the flight GOVERNOR SPIRO AGNEW of MARYLAND came to the airport to wish my mother and sister good future fortune. Years later, SPIRO AGNEW relocated himself to my town of RANCHO MIRAGE. His son was a regular at my business for a few seasons.

DAN QUAYLE. My ex and I worked at a tennis camp in VAIL, COLORADO. One of the player's parents was attending the camp and offered us a place to stay until our residence for the summer, and it was available. The large pad had a fabulous library. There were pictures throughout the house including that of VICE PRESIDENT DAN QUAYLE. Exploring the vast library, I discovered many books that were signed with warm wishes to DAN QUAYLE. We found out later that DAN QUAYLE was a partner in the ownership of the home. DAN QUAYLE admitted that he wanted to be recognized as the "BEST" golfer to ever grace 1600 PENNSYLVANIA AVENUE to ever represent the WHITE HOUSE, and HE WAS.

SENATORS: BARBARA BOXER. I had just finished shopping at COSTCO. I told my friend, "Heh, is that's SENATOR BARBARA BOXER eating pizza in the food court?" He said, "NO WAY." Earlier in the day, she had voted on the SENATE floor on an important bill. It was 8:00 p.m., and she was eating with her husband in the common eating area. I apologetically interrupted them to thank her for representing our state for all her years as a SENATOR. I shared with her that SENATOR TOM HARKIN of IOWA has visited my business for a few times. She inquired about my business and said, "I HAVE HEARD GREAT THINGS ABOUT YOUR BUSINESS AND KNEW I HAD BEEN OPERATING FOR A LONG TIME. SHE ASKED IF I WOULD LIKE A PICTURE.

BOB MONAGEN, SPEAKER OF THE CALIFORNIA ASSEMBLY. A pioneer of ENVIRONMENTAL ISSUES. He then became ASSISTANT OF THE SECRETARY OF TRANSPORTATION under RICHARD NIXON. He assisted me in the possibility of being a PAiGE in the UNITED STATES SENATE. He was my father's roommate and confidant at the COLLEGE OF PACIFIC, now the UNIVERSITY OF PACIFIC. He was an inspiration, and an influence in a young man's life. He died the same year as my father. I think of him often when I travel in CENTRAL CALIFORNIA due to that the INTERSTATE HIGHWAY is named after him.

SENATOR TOM HARKIN visited my business a few times with the leader of THE INDIAN TRIBE locally discussing the expansion of TRIBAL LAND BUSINESSES working with the government. He was engaging and enjoyed all of my sports memorabilia and meeting and occasional sports star. He had successful results here.

I was appointed to the "PRESIDENT'S COUNCIL of PHYSICAL FITNESS and the GOVERNOR'S COUNCIL of PHYSICAL FITNESS" by GOVERNOR ARNOLD SCHWARZENEGGER. An organization that most CALIFORNIA members were only there for "PHOTO OPS." NOT ME. I gave back to the community one-hundred plus percent. I visited and gave clinics to as many schools as possible and reaching out to tomorrow leaders. And the importance of participation in sports and community. I gave back and "NOT EXPECTING ANYTHING IN RETURN." I was blessed to achieve so much.

And talk about blessing, I was brought up CATHOLIC. "FATHER RYAN" was our family PRIEST, the PRIEST for UNITED STATES NAVAL ACADEMY FOOTBALL TEAM and later the DALLAS COWBOYS. ROGER STAUBACH. My father coined the phrase the opening of the roof of DALLAS COWBOY stadium was so "GOD COULD KEEP AN EYE ON HIS FAVORITE FOOTBALL PLAYER." FATHER RYAN would come and visit with a few other PRIESTS and stay at my parent's house to play golf. He always blessed me and prayed for me. All I know is they had great scores here on tough golf courses. One year, I visited VATICAN CITY during the summer. On this particular day, the POPE was giving mass to the public. I was wearing shorts which is a no-no to enter the church. I was only in VATICAN CITY for the day and did NOT want to pass up the opportunity to have mass with THE POPE, so I tried to mix in with the crowd to enter the church. THE SWISS GUARDS who have been protecting the VATICAN for centuries noticed my attire. I sprinted by them and into the church and was lost amongst the masses and got a seat in the church pews. THE POPE came within arm's length and blessed me and the others around me. I felt like I was touched by GOD!

little tid-bits

"RACE" came front and center at a young age.......returning home from OCEAN CITY, MARYLAND and asking my father "Why are those people in robes and burning a cross on that hill"? Dad responded "It's the KKK".......and he explained racism.......the woman who worked with us was a woman of color from the south.......and she took a day off to go to WASHINGTON, DC and hear the great speech of MARTIN LUTHER KING "I have been too the mountaintop".......on another return trip home my father wanted to educate us and drove through SELMA, ALABAMA and explained the SELMA CIVIL RIGHTS MARCH led my MARTIN LUTHER KING.......this was one week after the March.......my father always would educate us in numerous social settings.......VIETNAM unrest.......on our trip down to PALM SPRINGS my father took us to the burning down of the BANK OF AMERICA in SANTA BARBARA.......

"68" OLYMPICS in MEXICO CITY.......JOHN CARLOS, and TOMMIE SMITH protested on the podium raising their fists to the sky, black gloves on their hands, and heads bowed.......to protest peacefully about BLACK and RACISM.......JOHN CARLOS attended SAN JOSE STATE UNIVERSITY and with his free time helped coach the TRACK TEAM at PALO ALTO HIGH SCHOOL.......later in life he moved to the COACHELLA VALLEY and volunteered a local high schools for track.......

PRESIDENT RICHARD NIXON reached out to the REPUBLIC OF CHINA diplomatically to ease tensions and invited the NATIONAL PING PONG TEAM OF THE REPUBLIC OF CHINA for an exhibition and demonstration of their play at STANFORD UNIVERSITY, ROSCOE MAPLES PAVILLON.......these players would stand and play sometimes 30 feet away from the table and have these unbelievable rally's.......

ROSCOE TANNER and I were the "Marquee" names for the "BOY'S and GIRL'S CLUB" of ATLANTA, GEORGIA and hosted by the MAYOR ANDREW YOUNG and the city of ATLANTA, GEORGIA for "THE DOGWOOD FESTIVAL". We spoke at the nights festivities of a crowd of 1,000 in attendance.......ROSCOE gave me the mic and introduced me......."TRAINER, COACH, NUTIRIONIST, and CHEF" (unheard of at that time).......so the dignitaries, Mayor, Political figure's, etc.......about 40 went to the dinner at "RUTH CHRIS STEAKHOUSE".......when the server asked for my order......I said "PLAIN LETTUCE SALAD, 2 PLAIN POTATOES, and PLAIN VEGETABLES".......everyone went silent and listened to my order.......I played the game well......when we got back to our hotel suite I forced ROSOCE to go out and eat at midnight in BUCKHEAD and I ate everything on the menu.......

Another time Roscoe and I were scheduled to be the speakers at a tennis event at "SADDLEBROOK RESORT" in TAMPA, FLORIDA.......as we were boarding our flight ROSCOE turned to me and said "I'm NOT boarding the flight and will see you in a few days on our return flight too CALIFORNIA".......I said "Our event is NOT "RANDY" as the featured speaker, it's YOU, ROSCOE TANNER"?....... anyway I did a GREAT job!

O. J. SIMPSON.......I had two occasions interacting with O.J........ before the "???????".......at the airport (2 hours with ROSOCE TANNER, and at RIVERRA COUNTRY CLUB) both times he was narcistic and all the attention focused on him.......

JIM PUGH was the two-time defending mixed-doubles champion at the AUSTRALIA OPEN with the late JANA NOVATNA......30 minutes before the sign-in for an historic attempt for a three-peat she informed us "That she did not want to defend her titles".......JIM and I scrambled to find a playing partner.......I found NATASHA ZIEREVA and they went on to win the CHAMPIONSHIP over JIM'S doubles partner, RICK LEACH and ZINA GARRISON.......JIM and NATASHA also won WIMBLEDON MIXED DOUBLES CHAMPIONSHIP.......NATASHA presented me with a SOVIET UNION "SICKLE and HAMMER" T-shirt "Thanking me" for helping them win the CHAMPIOSHIPS.......

I was invited to play a charity golf event in LOS ANGELES with celebrities and athletes only at "MOUNTAIN BROOK COUNTRY CLUB".......pace of play was slow.......and backed up on the tee every hole......I noticed when I was teeing up for my start of the hole.......I would see "JOHNNY MATHIS" staring at me admiring my behind.......my playing partner said "JOHNNY" likes what he sees".......my behind.......I never knew he was gay.......

At the end of the year PLAYER'S NIKE TOUR CHAMPIONSHIP dinner I sat at the head table with TIM FINCHEM, my player, and six others.......included in our group was CASEY MARTIN who was suing the PGA TOUR for using a golf cart due to his medical condition.......I had empathy for CASEY having him play in our group during numerous tournaments.......he was a STANFORD grad and team player from my turf.......CASEY before each shot would say a verse from the bible.......TIGER WOODS was silent regarding supporting CASEY in his lawsuit.......CASEY MARTIN is a class act.......

LEFTY WILNER was a pioneer and legend in PAC 6, PAC 8 tennis. He had a career at UCLA, and in the professional ranks to have played BILL TILDEN, BOBBY RIGGS, to PETE SAMPRAS (read stories in tennis chapter about BILL TILDEN, BOBBY RIGGS, and PETE SAMPRAS.......our paths crossed on a regular basis for years........then I did not see LEFTY for about ten years.......then one morning he came into my business and had breakfast and paid his bill with quarters.......then a few days later he came in again and paid his breakfast bill with quarters.......then the next week he came in again and placed quarters on the counter where he sat.......my curiosity finally had to inquire "Why he had so many quarters"? LEFTY shared "He was living in a nursery home around the corner from my business and would get quarters from some of the homes residents" ....so I said "Come in anytime, and breakfast is on me"! He came in for another few months....... enjoyed meeting my guests, friends, and the tennis conversation....... he was a funny, engaging person who really did not have anyone to chat with....... he lived his last few months visiting daily and he died a few months later! SUPER GUY!!!!!!!

"MAKE the REST of YOUR life, the BEST of YOUR life" (JPS)

Made in the USA
Monee, IL
26 October 2022